Under the Moon

Program Authors
Richard L. Allington
Camille Blachowicz
Ronald L. Cramer
Patricia M. Cunningham
G. Yvonne Pérez
Constance Frazier Robinson
Sam Leaton Sebesta
Richard G. Smith
Robert J. Tierney

Instructional Consultant
John C. Manning

Program Consultant
Alice Parra

Critic Readers
Anita A. Ayala
Anne H. Ferrell
Pamela B. Houlares
Jesse Perry
Charlene H. Romero
Patsy K. Vittetoe

Scott, Foresman and Company

Editorial Offices:
Glenview, Illinois

Regional Offices:
Sunnyvale, California
Tucker, Georgia
Glenview, Illinois
Oakland, New Jersey
Dallas, Texas

Scott, Foresman Reading: An American Tradition

Acknowledgments

Text
Page 9: From the book *Moongame* by Frank Asch. Copyright © 1984 by Frank Asch. Published by Prentice-Hall, Inc., Englewood Cliffs, NJ 07632. Reprinted by permission.
Page 21: Adaptation of "The List" and illustrations on pp. 5–9, 11, 13, 14–17 from *Frog and Toad Together* by Arnold Lobel. Copyright © 1971, 1972 by Arnold Lobel. Reprinted by permission of Harper & Row, Publishers, Inc.
Page 31: Adapted by permission of Scholastic Inc. from *Night Animals* by Millicent E. Selsam. Copyright © 1979 by Millicent E. Selsam.
Page 35: Adapted text from *Norton's Nighttime*. Copyright © 1979 by Jane Breskin Zalben. All rights reserved. Reprinted by permission of Curtis Brown, Ltd. and Collins Publishers.
Page 41: "Night Comes" from *A Bunch of Poems and Verses* by Beatrice Schenk de Regniers. Text copyright © 1977 by Beatrice Schenk de Regniers. Reprinted by permission of Ticknor & Fields/Clarion Books, a Houghton Mifflin Company.
Page 42: Adapted from *Why the Sun and the Moon Live in the Sky* by Elphinstone Dayrell, illustrated by Blair Lent. Copyright © 1968 by Blair Lent, Jr. Reprinted by permission of Houghton Mifflin Company.
Page 57: Adaptation of complete text of *Through Grandpa's Eyes* by Patricia MacLachlan. Copyright © 1979 by Patricia MacLachlan. Reprinted by permission of Harper & Row, Publishers, Inc. and Curtis Brown Ltd.
Page 68: From "Abigail's Fingers" in *Fingers Are Always Bringing Me News* by Mary O'Neill. Copyright © 1969 by Mary O'Neill. Reprinted by permission of International Creative Management, Inc.
Page 69: Adapted and reproduced with permission of Four Winds Press, an imprint of Macmillan Publishing Company from *The Goat in the Rug* as told to Charles L. Blood and Martin Link by Geraldine, illustrated by Nancy W. Parker. Text: Copyright © 1976 by Charles L. Blood and Martin Link. Illustrations: Copyright © 1976 by Nancy Winslow Parker.
Page 99: Adaptation of entire text of *The Great Town and Country Bicycle Balloon Chase* by Barbara Douglass. Copyright © 1984 by Barbara Douglass. By permission of Lothrop, Lee & Shepard Books (A Division of William Morrow & Co.).

Continued on page 280

ISBN: 0-673-71507-8

Copyright © 1987,
Scott, Foresman and Company, Glenview, Illinois.
All Rights Reserved. Printed in the United States of America.

345678910-VHJ-96959493929190898887

Contents

9   Reading Warm-up

Moongame
Fantasy by Frank Asch

16   **Section One**
Looking Ahead:
Day and Night

1

Unit 1

18   Skill Lesson: Finding Order

21   A List   *Fantasy by Arnold Lobel*

Unit 2

31   Night Animals   *Informational article by Millicent Selsam*

35   Norton's Nighttime   *Fantasy by Jane Breskin Zalben*

41   Night Comes . . .
Poem by Beatrice Schenk de Regniers

Unit 3

42   Why the Sun and the Moon Live in the Sky
African folk tale retold by Elphinstone Dayrell

51   Looking Back
Thinking Skills
Writing: Sentences

52 Section Two
Looking Ahead:
Hands

2

Unit 4

54 Skill Lesson: Learning About Characters

57 Through Grandpa's Eyes
Realistic fiction by Patricia MacLachlan

68 *from* Abigail's Fingers   *Poem by Mary O'Neill*

Unit 5

69 The Goat in the Rug
*Fantasy by Geraldine as told to Charles Blood and
Martin Link*

Unit 6

81 Skill Lesson: Understanding r-controlled Vowels

84 Be Fit to Feel Good   *Health content-area reading*

88 Puppet Friends   *Informational article by Alan Bickley*

93 Looking Back
Thinking Skills
Writing: Sentences

94 Section Three
Looking Ahead:
Friends

3

Unit 7

96 Skill Lesson: Drawing Conclusions

99 The Great Town and Country
Bicycle Balloon Chase
Realistic fiction by Barbara Douglass

Unit 8

110 A Pet for Duck and Bear *Fantasy by Judy Delton*

123 Changing *Poem by Mary Ann Hoberman*

Unit 9

124 Stone Soup *French folk tale retold by Nancy Ross Ryan*

134 Looking Back
Thinking Skills
Writing: Sentences

135 Books to Read

| 136 | **Section Four**
Looking Ahead:
Time to Laugh | **4** |

Unit 10

138   Skill Lesson: Finding What It's All About

141   Pictures for Fun   *Informational article by Ruth Kaye*

146   Making People Laugh
Informational article by Thelma Gruenbaum

Unit 11

152   *from* "There are Rocks in My Socks!"
Said the Ox to the Fox
Choral reading by Patricia Thomas

156   The Golden Goose
Play from the story by the Brothers Grimm
adapted by Mary Shuter

Unit 12

163   Skill Lesson: Learning About Blends

165   Stormalong the Sailor
Tall tale retold by Mary Hynes-Berry

176   Fish Song   *Poem by Margaret Wise Brown*

177   Looking Back
Thinking Skills
Writing: Sentences

178 Section Five
Looking Ahead:
Birds

5

Unit 13

180 Skill Lesson: Learning About Goal and Outcome

183 The Magpie's Nest
English folk tale from English Fairy Tales,
collected by Joseph Jacobs

187 Goose Feathers *Realistic fiction by Emma L. Brock*

Unit 14

193 Sing, Mockingbird *Fantasy by Charnan Simon*

Unit 15

206 Birds Through the Year
Science content-area reading by Mary Hynes-Berry

210 Bird in a Hurry
Informational article by Joanne Bernstein

216 *from* Getting Ready *Poem by Aileen Fisher*

217 Looking Back
Thinking Skills
Writing: Sentences

218 Section Six
Looking Ahead:
Something Special

6

Unit 16

220   Skill Lesson: Learning About Maps and Globes

223   Too Many Books!   *Fantasy by Caroline Feller Bauer*

229   The Library
Social studies content-area reading by Sally Runck

234   Reading   *Poem by Marchette Chute*

Unit 17

235   Little Otter's Coasting Party   *Fantasy by Ann Tompert*

240   Best Friends   *Realistic fiction by Nancy Ross Ryan*

Unit 18

246   The Ugly Duckling
Tale by Hans Christian Andersen adapted by Nancy Ross Ryan

258   Looking Back
Thinking Skills
Writing: Friendly letter

259   Books to Read

260   Word Study Handbook

268   Glossary

277   Word List

Moongame

by Frank Asch

One day, Little Bird showed Bear a new game, hide and seek. First he told Bear to hide. He called out, "One, two, three, four, five, six, seven, eight, nine, ten." Then he went looking for Bear.

"I see you!" said Little Bird when he saw Bear hiding. "Now you try to find me!"

All day, Bear and Little Bird played their new game. When the sun went down, Little Bird went home.

It was late and only the moon was out. Bear looked up into the sky. He said to the moon, "Let's play a game! First I'll hide and you find me."

Then Bear ran as fast as he could. He ran to an old tree. Getting into the tree, he ducked down so the moon could not see him.

Bear sat for some time. Then he looked out from the tree. When he did, the moon was right there looking down at him.

"Good for you," said Bear. "You did find me. Now you go and hide."

Bear shut his eyes. He called out, "One, two, three . . . " just as Little Bird had.

Just then a light wind moved a big cloud. The cloud floated by the moon to hide it.

Bear called out "Ten." Then he set out to find the moon. At first it looked to Bear like the moon was hiding in a house.

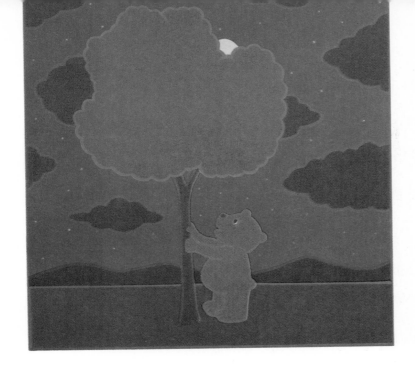

Next Bear saw the moon hiding in a tree.
He called, "I see you, Moon!" But Bear
was not right. All he could find was a
big balloon.

Then Little Bird came by to see Bear.

"Will you help me find the moon?" asked Bear.

"Yes, I'll help," said Little Bird.

Bear and Little Bird looked and looked. They could not find the moon. So they went to the woods to ask the animals for help.

"I don't think the moon can find his way back," said Bear. "Can you help me find him?"

"We will help you," said the animals.

Together they looked and looked. But they could not find the moon.

Bear was sad. He sat down and stopped to think. "Come back, Moon. The game is over," he said. "And I give up."

Just then the wind started to blow again. The moon came out of its hiding place.

"Look," said Little Bird. "The moon was hiding in back of that big cloud."

Bear was so happy he danced and danced. Then all the animals played hide and seek.

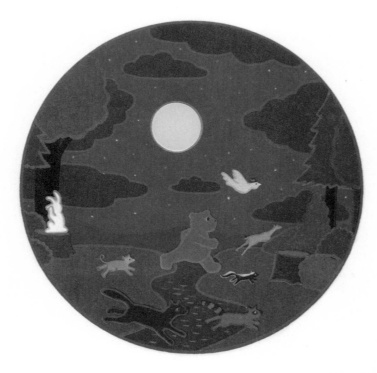

1

Day and Night

Many animals and birds live in the woods. Some of them move about all day. When the sky gets dark, the day animals go to sleep. The night animals come out to find something to eat.

Look at the pictures on pages 16–49. Find out what animals you will read about.

Finding Order

Imagine you want to tell your friend about a special day you had. You want to tell her by writing a note. Can you mail the note if you have not started to write it? No. First you have to write the note. Then, when it is set to be mailed, you can take it to the mailbox and mail it. You need to do things in the right order.

Things happen in order in your reading too. You learn what happens when you find out what happens first and what happens next. Some clue words can help you find the order. Read the next sentences. Look for any of the clue words *first, next, last, after,* and *then.* They will help you find out when things happen.

Rose had a good day today. First she had eggs for breakfast. Next she made a new friend at school. After school, Rose played a game with her mom. Then, when it got dark, Rose read a good book with her dad.

1. What happened first? What clue word helps you to know?

To find out what happened first, find the sentence that begins with *first*. The sentence tells you that Rose had eggs for breakfast.

2. What happened next? What clue word helps you to know?

To find out what happened next, find the sentence that begins with the clue word *next*. The sentence tells you that Rose made a new friend at school.

3. When did Rose play a game with her mom? What clue word begins the sentence?

4. What did Rose do when it got dark? Which sentence begins with *then*?

Practicing Time Sequence

Read the sentences to find out in which order things happen.

The sky was dark. It was night. First Cricket came out of his hiding place. Next he looked for something to eat. He saw some seeds and bugs and started to eat. Then Cricket played a noisy song.

1. What did Cricket do first? What clue word helps you to know?
2. What happened after Cricket had something to eat? What clue word helps you to know? .

Tips for Reading on Your Own

- As you read, look for clue words like *first, next, last, after,* and *then.*
- Think about the order in which things always happen. Does the order in which things happen in the story make sense?

A List

by Arnold Lobel

One morning Toad sat in bed. "I have many things to do," he said. "I will write them all down on a list so that I can remember them."

Toad wrote on some paper:

A List
of things to do
today

Then he wrote:

Wake up

"I already did that," said Toad, and he crossed out:

~~*Wake up*~~

Then Toad wrote other things on the paper.

A List
of things to do
today

~~Wake up~~
Eat breakfast
Get dressed
Go to Frog's house
Take walk
   with Frog
Eat
Take nap
Play games
   with Frog
Eat again
Go to sleep

"There," said Toad. "Now my day is all down on paper."

Toad got out of bed and had something to eat. Then he crossed out:

~~Eat breakfast~~

Toad got his clothes and got dressed.

Then he crossed out:

~~Get dressed~~

Toad put the list in his pocket. He opened the door and walked out into the morning.

Soon Toad was at Frog's door. He took
the list from his pocket and crossed out:

~~Go to Frog's house~~

Toad tapped on the door.

"Hello," said Frog.

"Hello. Look at my list of things to do,"
said Toad.

"Oh," said Frog, "I like that."

Toad said, "My list says that we will
go for a walk this morning."

"All right," said Frog. "Let's go."

Frog and Toad took a long walk. Then Toad took the list from his pocket again. He crossed out:

~~Take walk with Frog~~

Just then there was a huge wind. It blew the list out of Toad's hand. The list blew high, high up into the sky.

"Help!" shouted Toad. "My list is blowing away. What will I do without my long list?"

"Run fast!" said Frog. "We will run and reach high to catch it."

"No!" shouted Toad. "I can't do that."

"Why not?" asked Frog.

"Because," said Toad, "running after my list is not one of the things that I wrote on my list of things to do!"

Frog ran after the list. He ran over hills and swamps, but the list blew on and on.

At last Frog came back from a swamp.

"Hello, Toad," said Frog. "I am sorry, but I could not catch your list by the swamp."

"Oh no," said Toad. "I can't remember any of the things that were on my list of things to do. I will just have to sit here and do nothing."

Toad sat and did nothing. Frog sat with him.

After a long time Frog said, "Toad, it is getting dark. Soon it will be night. We must be going to sleep soon."

"Go to sleep!" shouted Toad. "Now I remember! That was the last thing on my list!"

Toad wrote on the ground with a stick:

Go to sleep

Then he crossed out:

~~Go to sleep~~

"There," said Toad. "Now my day is all crossed out!"

"I am so happy," said Frog.

Then Frog and Toad went right to sleep.

Meet the Author

Arnold Lobel wrote this story about Frog and Toad. He painted all the pictures too. When Mr. Lobel was a boy, he started drawing pictures. He told others about his pictures as he made up a story. Now he writes and draws pictures for many children's books.

Frog and Toad are Mr. Lobel's special friends. Read more about them in Frog and Toad Together and Frog and Toad Are Friends.

Checking Comprehension and Skills

Thinking About What You've Read

1. What happens to Toad's list?
2. Why does Toad make a list?
- 3. In the morning, what does Toad do after he has something to eat? What clue word helps you to know?
4. Why does Toad think he has to sit all day and do nothing?
- 5. What do Frog and Toad do after Toad's day is all crossed out? What clue word helps you to know?
6. Why do you think Toad likes Frog?

Talking About What You've Read

Toad made a list of things to do one day. Name some things you do in a day at school. Then tell which things you like to do. Tell why you like to do them.

Writing About What You've Read

Make a list of five things you do at school. Write them in the order that you do them.

- Comprehension: Time sequence

Night Animals

by Millicent Selsam

It is nighttime. You are sleeping in your bed. Many animals outside are sleeping too. Others are moving about. Let's see who is waking up.

A mouse steps out of its home. It looks for seeds to chew on. It looks for berries too.

The baby opossums are crawling all over their mother. Soon she will move them off. She will find something for her baby opossums to eat.

Some fruit would be good to eat. By now, the berries may be just right. If not, the mother may find some bugs for her baby opossums. Almost any little thing will do.

Five sets of yellow eyes shine in the moon's light. Five raccoons look for something to eat. They are on the way to a pond. There they will get some fish.

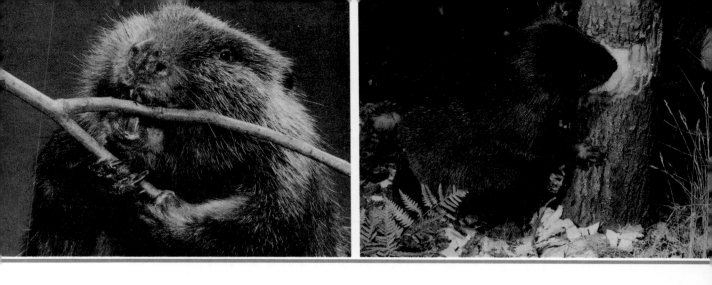

Beavers are working. They cut down
trees all through the night. One beaver
chews with its teeth on the branch of a
tree. The other beaver sticks its teeth into
a tree. It uses its teeth to chew through
the tree. At last the tree falls.

The porcupine sits high in a pine tree. Its quills look like pine needles. The porcupine smells some sweet berries. It will back down the tree. It will waddle over to the bushes. The berries are just right for eating. At the bush it will eat and eat.

The sky begins to get light. Night is over. The beavers will go back to their pond. The raccoons will go back to their tree. The porcupine will go up a tree. It will spread out on two branches.

All the night animals will find places to sleep. Then the sun will come up. The day animals will start to wake up. You will too.

Norton's Nighttime

by Jane Breskin Zalben

Norton is a raccoon. He lives in the woods. His home is under an old pine tree next to some bushes of berries. One day, late, Norton went for a walk. He did not see the sun crawl down through the trees. Norton was chilled as he sat in the still woods. He took a long look around. It was very dark. Norton could not see at all.

"Where am I?" Norton asked. "Where is the pine tree?"

Norton could hear noises in the night.
The wind blew through the moving trees.

"What do I hear? Is it just the wind?"
Norton asked. "Is something coming to
eat me?"

Norton could hear the leaves blowing
around. He was afraid. He started to sing
so he would not hear any noises.

"Who is coming closer and closer?" Norton
asked. He wanted to call for help. But he
was so afraid, no noise came out.

Trying not to be afraid, Norton asked,
"What would Possum do if she were here?"

He went up a tree and looked down. He
was very still, like Possum, so no one would
see him. But he fell out of the tree.

Almost crying, Norton said, "If Porcupine
were afraid, he would stick his quills out.
But I don't have quills. All I have is pine
needles. And I left them at home."

"What would Rabbit do if something
came after him?" Norton asked. "He would
hop away."

So Norton ran as fast as he could. He did not look where he was going. Just then he fell into a hole. He was so afraid. He could hear more noises. Something moved.

"Who is there?" Norton shouted. "C-come out where I can see you!"

A noise came out of the night.

"Norton?" it said.

"Possum, is that you I hear?" asked Norton.

"Yes, it's me," said Possum.

"And me," said Porcupine.

"And me," said Rabbit. "Oh, Norton, was that **you** making noise? We were so afraid."

Norton got out of the hole. "You think **you** were afraid," said Norton.

The animals walked back together through the woods. Norton said, "There is nothing to be afraid of. We are all friends."

"We are here if you need us," said Rabbit. He put his hand around Norton.

"Me, too," said Norton. "I'll be here."

Norton crawled under the pine branches. He wanted to sleep. In the moon's light, he floated off to sleep. If something were there in the nighttime, it had left.

Checking Comprehension and Skills

Thinking About What You've Read

1. What do the animals in "Night Animals" look for at night?
• 2. Put *will, waddle,* and *would* in ABC order.
3. In the story "Norton's Nighttime," why is Norton so afraid?
4. What does Norton do when he is afraid?
5. What can you do if you are afraid?
• 6. Put *bush, branch,* and *beaver* in ABC order.

Talking About What You've Read

Tell which animal you like reading about. Then tell why you like that animal.

Writing About What You've Read

Write three sentences about the animal you like reading about. Write why you like the animal.

• Study Skills: Alphabetical order

Night Comes...

by Beatrice Schenk de Regniers

Night comes
leaking
out of the sky.

Stars come
peeking.

Moon comes
sneaking,
silvery-sly.

Who is
shaking,
shivery-
quaking?

Who is afraid
of the night?

Not I.

Why the Sun and the Moon Live in the Sky

from the African folk tale retold by
Elphinstone Dayrell

At one time, the sun and water were very good friends. For many years, they lived on the earth together. Many times the sun would go to visit the water. But the water would not visit the sun.

The sun asked the water, "Why is it that you will not come to see me in my house?"

The water answered, "Your house isn't big enough. I have many people. If I came with all my people, I would push you out of your house. There is not enough room for us."

The water then said, "If you wish me to visit, you must build a large house. It must be a very large place. My fish and plants are many. They will need enough room to fit into your house."

The sun said, "Very well. I'll build a large house. It will have enough room for you and your people. Then you can visit me."

Soon after, the sun went home to his wife, the moon. He told her what he would do for the water. The moon said she would help.

The next day, the sun and moon began building a large house. They made it big so they could have visits from their friend. They worked many, long days to get the house done.

It took a long time to build the large house. When the house was done, the sun went to visit the water.

The sun began by saying, "Water, we have made a new house. It is large enough for you and your people. It took us until now to build it, but the house is done. Please come to visit."

The water answered, "I will. Thank you."

When the water went to the sun's house, one of his people asked, "Is it safe for the water to come in?"

The sun answered, "Yes, it is safe. Tell my friend to come in."

The water began to flow in. All of his fish, plants, and animals came too.

Very soon the water reached the sun's hands.

The water said, "You will get wet as I get deep. Is it still safe to come into your house? I don't want to push you out."

The sun again said, "Yes, do come in."

So more fish, plants, and water animals pushed their way through the door.

The water flowed in until it was as high as a man's head.

The water asked, "Am I getting too deep for you? Will I reach your heads? Do you want more of my people to come in?"

The sun and the moon both answered, "Come in." They did not know any better.

The water's people flowed on until the water was deep enough to reach the roof over the sun's and the moon's heads. The sun and moon did not want to get wet. So they moved up until they were on the roof.

Again the water said, "I still have more people left. Do you have room for them?"

Again the sun answered, "Yes, bring them in. Come in until there is no room left."

More of the water's people rushed in. They flowed in until there was no room left.

The water flowed over the top of the roof. So the sun and moon moved high into the sky, away from the earth. They did not get wet there. They lived away from the earth for years and years. And to this day, the sun and moon make their home in the sky.

Checking Comprehension and Skills

Thinking About What You've Read

- **1.** In this story, why do the sun and moon move to the sky?
- **2.** At the beginning of the story, why does the water not visit the sun?
- **3.** Why do the sun and the moon build a large house?
  4. If you were the water, what could you do to help the sun and the moon?
  5. What do the sun, moon, and water do in the story that could not happen?

Talking About What You've Read

Imagine you are telling a story about why the water lives on the ground. Make up your own story. Tell why the water does not live in the sky.

Writing About What You've Read

Write your story on paper. Tell why the water lives on the ground. Draw a picture to go with your story.

- Comprehension: Cause and effect relationships

LOOKING BACK

Thinking About the Section

First you read about Frog and Toad's day together. Then you read about night animals. Last you read a story about how the sun and the moon went to the sky. See if you can remember what happens in the day and night.

Writing About the Section

On your own paper, make two lists. Write the sentences that tell what happens in the day. Then write what happens at night.

Norton is afraid.
Toad's list blows away.
The moon comes out in the sky.
Beavers chew through branches.
Frog runs to catch the list.
The sun comes up.

Day	Night
1.	1.
2.	2.
3.	3.

2

Hands

There are many ways you can use your hands. You can touch things to find out what they feel like. You can make things. You may want to use your hands to play games and put on shows for people.

Look at the pictures on pages 54–92 to see what you will read about. Find some ways that people use their hands.

Learning About Characters

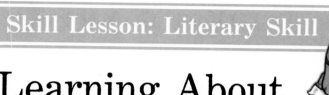

Look at the picture. Ann is with her pet dog, Prince. Ann takes Prince for a long walk after school. When Ann and Prince get home, Ann will get her dog some water to drink. You can tell from the picture that Ann likes Prince. She is smiling. You know Ann likes Prince because of the things she does for her pet.

As you read, you learn about the people and animals in a story. The people and animals are called the **characters.** Reading a story is more fun when you know about the characters. You can learn what characters are like by what they do. Pictures may give you clues about the characters too. Read the next paragraph. Find out what the boys do.

Ken and Bob are good friends. They work together to make a boat from wood. They put their boat in water. The boys try to make the boat float, but it does not float. The boys look the boat over. Ken and Bob are sad when they find a little hole in their boat.

1. Who are the characters in the paragraph?

Look for the names in the first sentence. Ken and Bob are the characters.

2. What do the boys do?

Find the sentence that tells that the boys work together. It says the boys make a boat.

3. What do the boys like to do? Look at the picture for a clue.

4. How do the boys feel when they find a hole in their boat? Why? Look at the last sentence and the picture for clues.

Practicing Story Elements: Character
Read to find out what Karen likes to do.

Karen painted a fall picture. First she painted a tree. Next she painted red, yellow, and orange leaves falling to the ground. When Karen's mom put Karen's painting up for her family to see, Karen said she likes painting.

1. Who is the character in the paragraph?
2. How does Karen feel about painting? Which sentence helps you to know?

Tips for Reading on Your Own
- Look for the names of the people and animals in the next story, "Through Grandpa's Eyes."
- As you read the story, find out what the characters do.
- Look at the pictures for clues about the characters.

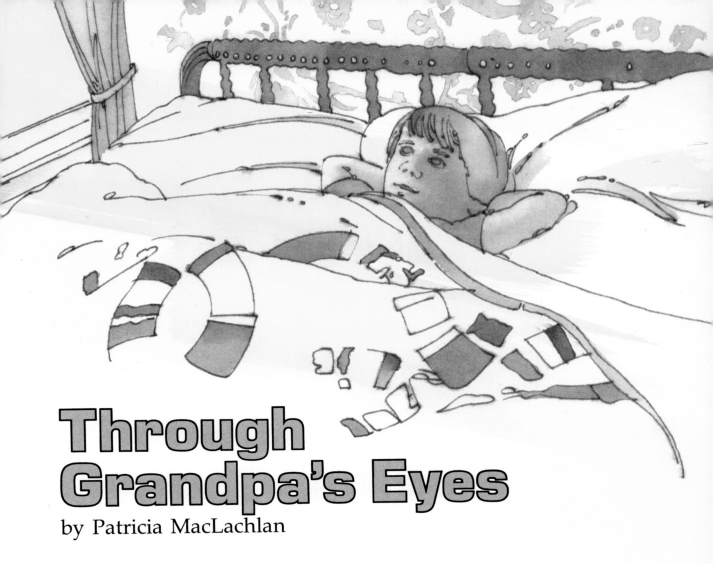

Through Grandpa's Eyes

by Patricia MacLachlan

My grandpa is blind. He does not see the way I do. He has his own way of seeing. When I visit Grandpa, I see through his eyes.

In the morning, I run to Grandpa's room. The sun wakes Grandpa in a different way than it wakes me. He says it touches him, waking him up.

When I look into his room, Grandpa is already up and doing his morning exercises. He stops and smiles because he hears me. Grandpa says, "Good morning, John."

I exercise with Grandpa, up and down. Then I try to exercise with my eyes closed. "One, two," says Grandpa, "three, four."

"Stop!" I say. I am still on one, two when Grandpa is on three, four.

"Breakfast!" calls Nana's voice from the kitchen.

"I smell eggs cooking," says Grandpa.
"Let's go down to the kitchen and eat."

I follow Grandpa down the steps. We go
into the kitchen. There are plates of food
set out for us.

Because Grandpa is blind, his plate of
food is like a clock. "Two eggs are at nine
o'clock," says Nana to Grandpa. "And the
bread is at two o'clock."

"Some honey," I tell Grandpa, "is at six
o'clock." I make my plate of food a clock,
too, and eat through Grandpa's eyes.

After breakfast, I follow Grandpa to the living room, to his cellos.

"Will you play with me, John?" he asks.

Grandpa tunes the cellos without looking. I play with a music stand and music next to me. I know all about the notes. I see them on the music. But Grandpa plays them. They are in his fingers. I close my eyes and play through Grandpa's eyes. My fingering hand slides up and down the cello. But I can't see how to play with my eyes closed.

"Listen," says Grandpa. "I'll play a tune I learned when I was only as old as you are. It was one I liked very much."

He plays the tune as I listen. That is the way Grandpa learns new songs, by listening.

"Now," says Grandpa. "Let's do it together."

"That is fine," says Grandpa as we play. "But play the right note, John," he calls to me. "Play the right note!"

After some time, Nana takes out her clay to make a shape of my grandpa's head. As Nana works, Grandpa takes out some wood. He calls it thinking wood, because he keeps it in his hand when he thinks. His fingers slide over the wood, making it smooth.

"May I have some thinking wood?" I ask.

Grandpa reaches into his pocket and gives me some wood. It feels smooth. My fingers slide over my thinking wood. I'll keep the wood in my pocket. Then when I am not at Grandpa's house, I can still think about Nana and Grandpa.

When Nana is done working, Grandpa runs his hand over the clay, his fingers smooth and quick. "It looks like me," he says.

My eyes have already told me that it looks like Grandpa. But he shows me how to feel his face with my fingers. Then he shows me how to feel the clay face.

My fingers flow down the clay face and under the eyes. It does feel like Grandpa. This time my fingers tell me.

After Grandpa and I take a walk by the river, Nana calls us for lunch. "Nana has made hot bread for lunch," Grandpa says. I close my eyes. All I can smell is the wet earth by the river as we walk back.

After lunch, the three of us take books outside to read under a tree. Because he is blind, Grandpa reads his book with his fingers. The book has many dots. Grandpa feels the dots. The dots tell him the words.

Grandpa reads something funny and laughs. "Read what is so funny," says Nana. And he does. Nana and I listen to the funny story. A squirrel in the tree looks like he is listening too. But Grandpa can't see him.

At night, after we eat, the sky gets dark. In some way, Grandpa knows when it is dark, and he walks with me up the steps to bed. I get into bed. Grandpa reaches down to kiss me, his hands feeling my head.

"It feels like you need a cut, John," he says.

As Grandpa leaves me with a kiss, he puts out the light by my bed. But what he does not know is that he has put the light on. After Grandpa closes the door, smiling, I get up to put out the light.

When it is dark for me the way it is dark for Grandpa, I hear the night noises that Grandpa hears. I hear the birds sing their last songs of the day. "Grandpa," I call, wanting him to listen too.

"I hear," he calls back.

"Go to sleep, John," says Nana.

Grandpa says her voice smiles to him. I want to find out. "What?" I call to Nana.

"I said go to sleep," she answers. Nana says it as if I must go to sleep now. But Grandpa is right. Her voice smiles to me. I know. Because I look through Grandpa's eyes.

Checking Comprehension and Skills

Thinking About What You've Read

- 1. What does John learn about through Grandpa's eyes?
2. When Grandpa eats, how does he know where the food is on his plate?
- 3. What does Nana like to do?
- 4. Why do you think John likes Grandpa?
5. In the story, Grandpa smells hot bread. What foods can you name by smelling them?

Talking About What You've Read

Imagine you have some honey in your hand. What would it feel like in your hand? Would it feel wet or smooth? In a word, tell how some other things would feel in your hand: honey, some clay, a cello, a squirrel, and Grandpa's book.

Writing About What You've Read

On the left side of your paper, write the names of the things you told about. On the right side, write a word that tells what they would feel like in your hand.

- Literary Skills: Character

Abigail's Fingers

by Mary O'Neill

One day Abigail said
In surprise:
"My fingers are almost
The same as my eyes.
Fingers are always
Bringing me news
Toes never know
Because of shoes.
They tell me what
Is hot and cold,
And what is too heavy
For me to hold.
They tell me what
Is soft and hard
And help me write
A postal card.
They know the rough
Of brick and log
And that the softest thing
Is fog."

The Goat in the Rug

by Geraldine
as told to Charles Blood and Martin Link

My name is Geraldine. I am a goat. I live close to a place called Window Rock. I live there with my friend, Glenmae. The rock is called Window Rock because it has a big hole in it. The hole looks like a window open to the sky.

I call my friend Glenmae. That is because I can't say her Indian name, Glee´Nasbah, very well. Glenmae likes to weave. I think that is why, one day, she wanted to weave me into a rug.

I remember it was a hot day. The sun was out. At first I did not know what was happening. I was on the ground. Glenmae was cutting off my wool in long pieces. I did not feel a thing, but I could not stay still. I laughed as she cut my wool.

I may have looked a little funny after
that, but my, did I feel good! I wanted
to stay around and see what would
happen next.

The first thing Glenmae did was chop
up a special plant. She chopped it into
pieces. The pieces made a good soap.
She put them into a pail of water. She
cleaned my wool in the soap until it was
clean and white. After that, a little of me
(you could say) was hung up in the sun.

After some time, Glenmae took out two large combs. The combs had many teeth. Glenmae combed each piece of my wool. She told me it made a smooth yarn for spinning.

Then Glenmae started to spin my wool into yarn. I was beginning to find out it takes a long time to make a rug. Again and again, Glenmae shaped and pulled, shaped and pulled the wool. Then she started spinning each piece around a long stick. She was shaping, pulling, and spinning the yarn. It began to look fine and smooth.

Some days passed. Glenmae and I got a
pail. We went for a walk. Glenmae said
we were going to find some special
plants. She would use them to make dye.

I did not know what "dye" was. I was
thinking it could be something to eat. I do
like to eat plants. But that is why
Glenmae got mad at me. As Glenmae was
looking for plants, I was eating each one
she had in the pail. How good they were!

The next day, Glenmae made me stay
home. She walked a long way to buy
some dye. She said it would not be as
good as the dye she makes from plants.
But because I was such a pig, it would
have to do.

I was afraid that Glenmae would still be
mad at me when she got back. But she
was not. Soon she had made three big
pots of dye. Each pot got very hot as the
dye cooked.

Then I saw what Glenmae had told me
about dyeing. She dipped my white wool
into one pot. It turned pink! She dipped
it in again. The color did not stay pink.
My wool began to turn dark pink! When
Glenmae was done dipping my wool in
and out, she hung it up. By that time it
had turned a deep red.

After that, Glenmae dyed some of my
wool brown. She dyed some of it black.
I could not help but think if I would turn
colors after eating all of the plants.

As I was thinking, Glenmae started to make our rug. She took a ball of yarn. She began winding it around and around two poles. I don't know how many times she had to wind it, because I was still thinking. I was afraid of what it would be like to be the only red, white, black, and brown goat at Window Rock.

Soon Glenmae was done winding the yarn. Then she hung the poles on a big stand of wood. She called the stand a loom.

After seven days of getting set to weave, Glenmae started our rug. She began weaving one piece of yarn at a time. Our rug started growing to the top of the loom. Some pieces of black. Some of brown. Some of red. In and out. Right and left went the yarn, until, soon, we could see our rug taking shape.

Our rug did not grow fast. As always, Glenmae made a rug that was different from any other rug.

Then, at last, our weaving was done!
But first I had to look it over. I looked at
one side. Then I looked at the other side.
Only then did I let Glenmae take our rug
off the loom.

There was so much of me in that rug. I
wanted it to be just right. And it was.

Now, again, my wool is almost long
enough for Glenmae and me to make a
new rug. I want to very soon. You see,
there are not many people left who weave
like Glenmae. And there is only one goat
like me, Geraldine.

Meet the Illustrator

Nancy Winslow Parker did the drawings for
"The Goat in the Rug." Ms. Parker has
always liked to draw. She makes her pictures
funny.

Ms. Parker likes dogs. She wrote a book called
Poofy Loves Company, about one of her dogs.
For fun, Ms. Parker likes to grow plants, take her
dogs to dog shows, and make things from wood.

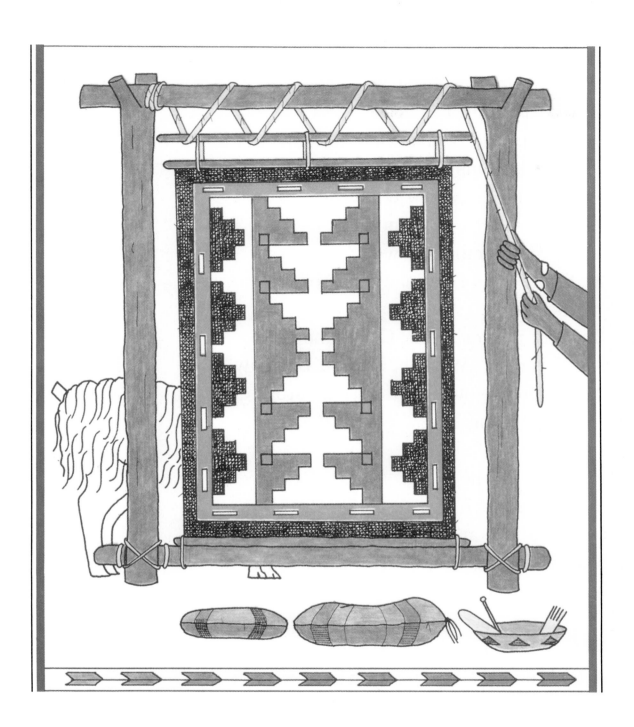

Checking Comprehension and Skills

Thinking About What You've Read

- **1.** Put in order what Glenmae does.
    - a. She spins the wool.
    - b. She cleans the wool.
    - c. She dyes the wool.
    - d. She combs the wool.
- **2.** What does Glenmae do after she winds the yarn?
  - **3.** Why do you think Geraldine likes Glenmae? What helps you to know?
  - **4.** What do you like about the story "The Goat in the Rug"? Why?

Talking About What You've Read

Look at each picture from the story. Imagine you are Glenmae telling the story. Tell what you would say to Geraldine in each picture.

Writing About What You've Read

Pick one picture from the story. Write what Glenmae could be saying to Geraldine in the picture. Then write what Geraldine could answer.

- Comprehension: Steps in a process

Understanding r-controlled Vowels

The children are playing a ball game. They each try to hit a ball around a playing field. Look at the letters and words on the colored balls. In each word, the vowel is followed by the letter *r*. Read the words. Can you tell which sound each vowel stands for when it is followed by the letter *r*?

ar
car

or
for

er
her

ur
turn

ir
bird

When a vowel is followed by the letter *r*, it does not have a long sound. It does not have a short sound. The *r* following the vowel changes it to an r-controlled vowel sound.

The letters *ar* stand for the vowel sound you hear in the word *car*. The letters *or* stand for the vowel sound you hear in the word *for*.

The vowels *e*, *i*, or *u* followed by the letter *r* all stand for the same sound. You hear this sound in the words *her*, *bird*, and *turn*. Now read some new words.

barn	horn	herd	skirt	hurt

Which word has the vowel sound you hear in the word *car*? (barn) What word has the vowel sound you hear in *for*? (horn) Which words all have the same vowel sound? (herd, skirt, and hurt) What different letters stand for that one r-controlled vowel sound? (*-er*, *-ir*, and *-ur*)

Practicing r-controlled Vowels

Read what Joe does for his team. Six words have r-controlled vowel sounds. After you read, find the six words that have the same vowel letters and vowel sounds as the words *car*, *her*, *for*, *girl*, and *turn*.

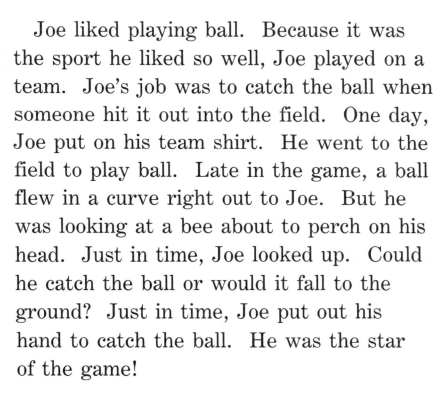

Joe liked playing ball. Because it was the sport he liked so well, Joe played on a team. Joe's job was to catch the ball when someone hit it out into the field. One day, Joe put on his team shirt. He went to the field to play ball. Late in the game, a ball flew in a curve right out to Joe. But he was looking at a bee about to perch on his head. Just in time, Joe looked up. Could he catch the ball or would it fall to the ground? Just in time, Joe put out his hand to catch the ball. He was the star of the game!

Tip for Reading on Your Own

- If a word has a vowel followed by the letter *r*, try the sounds you hear in *car*, *her*, and *for*.

Be Fit to Feel Good

Every day you do many things. You go to school, read and work, and eat and play. You need to feel good to do the things you do. If you are **fit,** you feel good and look good. You eat good foods and get enough sleep. You get enough exercise to stay in shape.

Eating Well

Every day you need to eat different kinds of foods to stay well. You need milk and foods made from milk, because milk helps you grow. Fruit, bread, and fish are good things to eat too. Eating a good breakfast each day helps you start your day right.

Getting Enough Sleep

After a day of work and play, you need a good night's sleep. Then you can wake up feeling good the next morning. You need enough sleep every night to do a good job at school reading, thinking, and listening.

Exercising to Keep Fit

There are many ways to get **exercise.** Some children like to run or swim to get exercise. Other children like to play games. They may like sports or playing on a team.

Jan and Rob both like sports. They use their hands as they play their sports. Jan plays on a ball team every Saturday. Each Saturday she puts on her team shirt. Jan's shirt helps people know which team she is on. Jan uses a bat to hit the ball. She gets exercise by running to home plate.

Rob uses his hands in a different kind of sport. He likes to bowl each Saturday. Rob and his friends try to hit the pins with the bowling ball. Then Rob and his friends ride their bikes home. They get exercise by riding their bikes and bowling.

Some children like to dance, jump, or move in different ways. They use their hands as they turn and jump. They get exercise by dancing, jumping, and moving. The children practice every day to do well. They like to show others what they can do.

Staying Fit

What kind of exercise do you get? How can you stay fit? Plan a way to get exercise every day. Eat the right kinds of foods and get enough sleep. Then you will feel good, have fun, and stay fit.

Puppet Friends

by Alan Bickley

Puppets are fun to make and use. They
may look like funny animals or people.
Without the people who make them talk and
move, puppets are just faces and costumes.

Some people work with puppets every
day. Some of them make the puppets.
Some work with the puppets to put on
puppet shows. The people use their voices
to make the puppets talk. They move the
puppets. The puppets tell a story.

There are many kinds of puppets. One kind is a hand puppet. You use your fingers to make the puppet turn, move, and talk. Make a hand puppet of your own.

1. Get a box and cut a line through three sides. Put your fingers in the top. Practice moving the mouth to talk.
2. Put colored paper all around the box.
3. Cut out two eyes from paper. Add them to the box. Now your puppet has a face.
4. Cut out two curves from red paper. The curves will be the puppet's lips. Add the lips to its face.
5. Cut some yarn for the hair. What color will the hair be? Add the hair to its head. Make your puppet move and talk!

You can make this puppet too.

Stick puppets have a stick on them. To move the puppet, the people place their hands just under the stage. They move the stick. The puppet moves around the stage.

Some puppets are hung from lines over the stage. The people who work the puppets stand over the stage. No one sees them as they pull the lines. When the people pull and turn the lines, the puppets dance, jump, or perch on things. Sometimes the puppets look funny as they move about!

A different kind of puppet can be big. Someone dresses in a costume to look like an animal. The costume hides who is in it.

Other puppets have poles on their hands. Someone moves this puppet's hands by pushing and pulling the poles.

After much practice, it is time for a puppet show. Many people come to see it. They listen to the funny puppets talk. After the show, the real stars of the show tell about their puppet friends. The stars are the people who make puppets special.

Checking Comprehension and Skills

1. In "Be Fit to Feel Good," what are some ways to stay fit?
2. What sport or game do you like to play?
- 3. In the sentence "Then Rob and his friends ride their bikes home," from "Be Fit to Feel Good," which people ride bikes?
4. How do you know that some people like puppets?
5. Which kind of puppet do you like?
- 6. In the sentence, "The people use their voices to make the puppets talk," from "Puppet Friends," which voices make the puppets talk?

Talking About What You've Read
You have read many words that tell how children and puppets move. *Jump* and *dance* are two of them. Name some others.

Writing About What You've Read
Make a list of words that tell ways to move. Write two sentences using some of the words.

- Comprehension: Referents

LOOKING BACK

Thinking About the Section

You have read about ways people use their hands. Grandpa learned about things around him. Glenmae made a rug. Children played sports and games. Some people made puppets.

Writing About the Section

On your own paper, match the characters with the ways they used their hands.
The sentences you write will tell what the characters did. You may need to write two sentences about some of the characters.

Grandpa	made a rug.
John	made puppets.
Nana	did exercises.
Glenmae	put on a puppet show.
Rob	played a sport.
Jan	made a clay face.
The puppet people	played a cello.

Read your sentences. Which sentences could tell about you?

3

Friends

Some people are your friends for a long time. New friends are people you meet and learn about. Friends share, work together, and do kind things for each other.

Look through pages 96–133 to see what people and animals you'll read about. Look for pictures of great friends together.

Drawing Conclusions

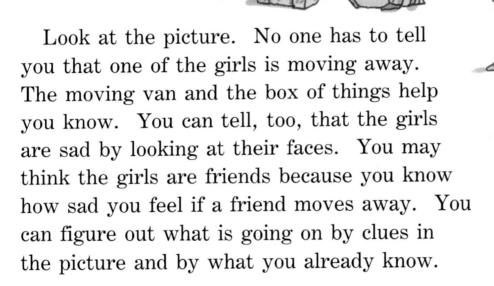

Look at the picture. No one has to tell you that one of the girls is moving away. The moving van and the box of things help you know. You can tell, too, that the girls are sad by looking at their faces. You may think the girls are friends because you know how sad you feel if a friend moves away. You can figure out what is going on by clues in the picture and by what you already know.

When you read, some things are not said in the story or article. You need to find clues that help you figure out what characters are like and what is happening. Read the next paragraph. Look for clues that help you know what Ed and Mr. Vega will do.

Ed gets his pole and a pail. He stops
to see Mr. Vega, his friend. Ed asks
Mr. Vega if he would like to go to the
lake. Each time the two of them go, they
have fun. First they dig in the ground to
get what they need. Mr. Vega gets his
pole. Then they walk to the lake.

1. What are Ed and Mr. Vega going to do?
   What helps you to know?

They are going fishing. You can tell
because they have poles to fish with and a
pail to put the fish in. They dig in the
ground to get what they need, and they
walk to the lake.

2. How do you know Mr. Vega and Ed are
   friends? What three clues help you?

Ed asks Mr. Vega if he would like to go
to the lake. The two have walked to the lake
other times. They have fun when they go.

3. What do Mr. Vega and Ed dig for? Think
   about what they need to catch fish.
4. How do you know the lake is close by?
   Read how they get there.

Practicing Drawing Conclusions

Read the paragraph and try to figure out where the friends are.

I like to come here with Mom and my friend Jill to see the animals. I like the big, white bears. I like to see them swim and play. My friend Jill likes to look at the big birds. Mom likes one bird with colored feathers. Jill and I get balloons to take home. We have fun when we go to see the animals and birds.

1. Where are the friends?
2. What clues help you to know?

Tips for Reading on Your Own

- Think about what you read in the next story. Find clues that help you figure out what is happening.
- When you read, use what you already know to figure out what is not said in the story.

The Great Town and Country Bicycle Balloon Chase

by Barbara Douglass

"What is a bicycle balloon chase?" Gina asked Grandpa. It was the second time she had read about it that week.

They went to see the man in town who worked on bikes. He told Gina and Grandpa all about it.

The man said, "A big hot air balloon will be launched in the park this Saturday. Only the wind knows which way it will go. We will follow it on our bikes. After the balloon hits the ground, the first two people who get close enough to touch it will get a ride in the balloon."

That week Gina and Grandpa biked all over town. They biked up hills. They biked down hills. Grandpa wanted to see how many shortcuts they could find. He said, "If only the wind knows which way the balloon will go, we have to know every shortcut."

On Saturday Gina and Grandpa were up
before the sun. After breakfast Grandpa got
their bikes ready. At last he put on his cap
and said, "Let's go chase that balloon."

On the way to the park Gina saw cars with
bicycles on the front. She saw cars with
bicycles on the back. She saw cars with
bicycles on the top, but she did not see
a balloon.

In the park Gina saw all different kinds
of bicycles, but she did not see a balloon.
She saw a woman with a bird. The woman
was standing by the back of a van.

"Where is the balloon?" asked Gina.

"Look in the back of that van," Grandpa told her. "The balloon is in the bag."

"I thought it would be a great BIG balloon," said Gina.

"It will be," said Grandpa. "Just keep looking."

Gina looked on. The woman and her helpers opened the bag. They pulled out a huge balloon of green, red, purple, and blue. They rolled out the balloon. They rolled it out and rolled it out until the balloon spread over the ground.

The long balloon had a big mouth. The
helpers worked to keep the mouth open. The
woman turned on a fan. The balloon started
growing. Next the woman turned on a burner.
Hot air blew into the balloon. The balloon
started growing more and more. At last it
was standing up tall. It was as tall as ten
buildings put on top of each other. It was
ready to be launched.

"Ready?" called the woman.

"Ready!" answered the people on bikes.

The helpers let go of the ropes. The
balloon floated up and away.

After the balloon was launched, nobody could tell which way to go. One man thought, "The wind will blow the balloon this way. Let's go this way."

A woman thought, "The wind will blow the balloon that way. Let's go that way."

Grandpa took a shortcut. He started out in front. Gina followed Grandpa. When the balloon floated this way, Grandpa took this shortcut. When the balloon floated that way, Grandpa took that shortcut. Gina followed Grandpa through every shortcut in town.

The balloon floated down. Gina and Grandpa followed it into the country. They followed it past this farm and that farm. The balloon made the farm animals afraid.

Then the balloon floated closer to the ground, in an open field. "Quick, quick," said Gina. "Nobody is here. Let's touch the balloon. I think we could be first!"

The woman looked out in front. Bees flew around the balloon. She called, "Oh, no! Bees! We will have to look for a better place." Hot air from the burner made the balloon go up again.

Grandpa and Gina biked on. When the balloon dipped in front of them a second time, Grandpa and Gina were ready to run and touch it.

Before the two reached the balloon, the woman called, "Oh, no! A bull! We will have to look for a better place."

The burner started again. The bull gave out a cry. The woman's bird called out, afraid of the bull. Then the bird flew.

The woman called, "Oh, no! Gypsy! You come back here!"

Gypsy flew this way. The balloon blew that way. Gina followed Gypsy. Grandpa followed Gina. Nobody followed Gina and Grandpa. All the other people on bikes followed the balloon. The bird did not take any shortcuts. It flew right through the country, all the way around the farms before it stopped on a tall plant. Gina reached up and caught it.

Gina and Grandpa turned their bikes around. They biked as fast as they could. They biked past the farms a second time.

Gina and Grandpa were the last ones to reach the balloon. The first two people who had touched the balloon were ready to take their ride. The hot air balloon pulled at the ropes. Gypsy flew back to the woman.

Just then the woman called to her helpers, "Stop! Don't let go yet." She called to Gina and Grandpa. She said, "Please put your bicycles in the van and come over here. There is room here for two more people. Any people who can catch my bird must have a ride in my balloon."

What a great ride they had!

Checking Comprehension and Skills

Thinking About What You've Read

1. Do Gina and Grandpa touch the balloon first? Why or why not?
2. How do Gina and Grandpa practice for the bicycle balloon chase?
• 3. Why do you think Gina follows the bird?
• 4. How do you know that the woman is happy to have her bird back?
5. Would you like to take a ride in a hot air balloon? Why or why not?

Talking About What You've Read

Imagine you are in a hot air balloon. Tell how things look from up in a balloon. Then tell how things look from your bike as you ride on the ground.

Writing About What You've Read

Imagine that you take a ride in a hot air balloon. Write about what you see from the balloon. Tell what you like about your ride.

• Comprehension: Drawing conclusions

A Pet for Duck and Bear

by Judy Delton

"Duck, Duck!" called Bear, tapping at the door. "I have a surprise for you."

Duck came to the door. He had been cleaning the house.

"First, I want to thank you for the canary you gave me, Duck," said Bear. "He is a fine pet."

Duck said, "Yes, Bear. He is just the pet I would have wanted. He is little and clean, and stays in a cage and sings all day. What is the surprise you have?"

"I have something for you, too, Duck.
Close your eyes," said Bear.

Bear went around to the side of the
house. When he came back he had a long
rope. Tied to the rope was a large dog.

Bear said, "I thought you would like a
pet too, Duck. And I got you the kind of
pet I would like to have. I said when I
saw him, 'This is Duck's dog.' He will be a
fine friend for you, Duck."

Duck opened his eyes. He looked up at
the dog. It was taller than Duck. The dog
put a foot on Duck.

"Oh, Bear, this is a very large dog. He is taller than I am," said Duck.

"He will be a fine friend, Duck. And a good watchdog," said Bear.

The dog jumped through the middle of the room, tipping over things. Duck rushed to catch things that he did not want to fall over.

"He is a fine jumping dog, Duck," said Bear.

Then Bear started on his way home.

"Well," said Duck, "I have never had a dog before."

The dog was hungry, so he went into Duck's kitchen and started eating Duck's food.

"Oh my," said Duck, trying his hardest to be kind. "This dog has no manners."

The next day Duck went to Bear's house for a visit.

Bear said, "Come in, come in! How is your dog, Duck? How is Ducksdog?"

Duck thought. "He is much taller than me," said Duck. "And he has no manners."

Bear felt sad that the dog had no manners.

"He is a fine pet," Duck was quick to say. "He is a good watchdog, Bear."

Bear smiled. "I thought you would like him," he said.

Bearsbird was flying around the room. He came to sit on Duck.

Duck asked, "Bear, why isn't your canary in a cage? A canary belongs in a cage."

Bear gave Duck a piece of honey cake and a cup of tea. He set out a plate of dog biscuits for Bearsbird. The canary flew down to the table and began to pick at one.

"I don't think Bearsbird likes to be in a cage, Duck. He likes to fly, you know." Bear gave himself some tea. "I have been showing him how to do tricks."

"Tricks?" said Duck. "A canary does not do tricks, Bear. A canary is a singer."

"You may be right," said Bear. "It has been the hardest thing to do. I have had the hardest time getting him to roll over and play dead."

"Play dead!" said Duck, surprised. "A dog can learn to play dead, but never a canary. A canary is a singer, not a dog. Dog biscuits are not good for him, Bear. Bird seeds are better for birds."

Duck ate his cake and left for home.

On his way home, Duck said to himself, "Bear is not doing good things for Bearsbird. I never did hear of a canary that ate dog biscuits."

The following week, Bear was on the way home from buying more dog biscuits. He stopped at Duck's house. "I have come to see Ducksdog," he said.

"Come in, come in," said Duck. "He has just had his bath."

Ducksdog was sitting in a big cage in the middle of the room. His hair was brushed and shining. There was a red tie in it. He looked sad.

"Come and have some tea," said Duck.

The two friends sat down at the table.
Duck gave Bear some tea and cut three
pieces of seed cake. He put two on the
table and one in a big, red bowl. He set
the bowl down for Ducksdog.

"Here, Ducksdog!" called Duck, opening
the door to the cage.

Ducksdog came out. The dog walked to
his bowl and sniffed at the cake.

The two friends ate their cake together.
After Ducksdog ate some cake, he went
back into his cage and sat down. He put
his head down because he felt sad.

When Bear was done eating his cake, he
left for home.

Bear said, "That dog is not himself. He
is not the same happy dog I know.
He needs to run and jump outside. He
must be hungry for a good dog biscuit."

What do you think Bear will do next?

The next morning Duck tied the rope on
the dog and set off for Bear's house. When
Duck was in the middle of the woods, he
saw Bear. Bear had a bird cage with Bearsbird
in it.

"Why, hello there, Bear. I was just on my
way to your house," said Duck.

Bear said, "And I was coming to your
house, Duck. I have been thinking about our
pets. I think Bearsbird belongs with you.
You have always wanted a canary, Duck."

Duck said, "And you have always wanted
a dog for a pet. Ducksdog is not happy
staying with me. His tail never moves and he
is sad."

Bear handed the cage to Duck. Duck handed the rope to Bear. Then Duck said, "Now Ducksdog is Bearsdog! He belongs to you. He is a fine watchdog, Bear!"

Bear said, "And Bearsbird is Ducksbird! He is a fine singer, you know, Duck."

Then the two friends each went home with their new pets.

Meet the Author

Judy Delton wrote this story about Duck and Bear. She thinks she is like Duck and Bear in some ways. Mrs. Delton first started writing books when she wanted a job trying something new. She was surprised when children liked what she wrote. Now she writes many books for children.

Checking Comprehension and Skills

Thinking About What You've Read

1. How do Duck and Bear get pets that they like?
2. How do you know that Duck does not know very much about dogs?
- 3. What did you think Bear would do when he saw how sad the dog was? Were you right?
4. How do you know that Duck and Bear are friends?
- 5. Do you think the pets will be happy in their new homes? Why or why not?

Talking About What You've Read

Both Duck and Bear gave each other a pet they would have wanted. Tell which pet you would like for a pet, a dog or a canary. Then tell why you would want it.

Writing About What You've Read

Make a list of things you could do for a pet dog or canary so it would be a happy pet.

- Comprehension: Predicting outcomes

Changing

by Mary Ann Hoberman

I know what *I* feel like;
I'd like to be *you*
And feel what *you* feel like
And do what *you* do.
I'd like to change places
For maybe a week
And look like your look-like
And speak as you speak
And think what you're thinking
And go where you go
And feel what you're feeling
And know what you know.
I wish we could do it;
What fun it would be
If I could try you out
And you could try me.

STONE SOUP

retold by Nancy Ross Ryan

One cold day, in a place far away, three soldiers were walking together. The soldiers had been walking a long time. They were very hungry.

"How I would like to get some good food to eat!" said the first soldier.

"A bed to sleep in too," said the second.

"Then we must walk on," said the last.

They walked a little faster. Just then, in front of them, they saw the lights of a village.

"We may find something to eat there," said the first soldier.

"A place to sleep too," said the second.

"We will share what we find," said the third.

Now the people in that village were afraid of people they did not know.

"Oh, oh," they said. "Here come three soldiers. We know how soldiers are. They are always hungry. We have little enough food for us."

So the people ran to hide their food. They hid every last bit.

They pushed bags of potatoes under the straw. They put pails of milk down the wells. They spread old sheets over the carrots. They hid all their meat. Then they went inside their houses and closed their windows and doors.

The soldiers first stopped at the house of Anne and Robert.

"Hello," the first soldier said. "Could you share a bit of food with three hungry soldiers?"

"Sorry," the man and woman said. "We are hungry too. Our family has had nothing to eat for three days. It has been a bad year for farmers." Then they shut the door.

The soldiers went on to the next house, which belonged to Paul and Marie.

"Could you share a bit of food?" the second soldier asked Marie.

"Some straw will do for the night," said the third.

"We are sorry," said Marie. The soldiers who came before you ate everything we had to give."

"The animals ate all the straw," said Paul.

At every house people said the same thing. Nobody had any food to give away. People got together in the middle of the village and looked as hungry as they could.

The three soldiers talked together. "No use talking about it," said the first soldier. "We will have to make stone soup."

"Stone soup?" thought the people. Everyone wanted to see stone soup being made.

"First, we will need a large pot," one soldier said.

The people got as large a pot as they could find.

"Now, some water to put into the pot and wood to cook with," said the soldiers. People came running with pails of water and wood.

"Now, we must add three smooth stones," said the last soldier.

Everyone helped to find the stones.

"Stones like this can make good soup," said the first soldier, as he began to stir the soup. "But a really great stone soup needs carrots."

"Why, I just remembered," said Anne, "I think I put a carrot or two away," and off she ran. She came back with the carrots she had been hiding.

"If we only had a bit of meat and some potatoes," said the next soldier.

"I saw some potatoes under some straw the other day," said a man. "What they were doing there, I'll never know." Off he ran to get them.

He came back with the potatoes. A second man came back with some meat he had been hiding. The soldiers cut up the meat and potatoes and put them in the soup.

"Oh," said one soldier as he stirred, "a cup of milk would make this soup fit for the queen. Come to think of it, that is just what she asked for when she last ate with us. No use asking for what you don't have," he said, and looked around.

"Well!" the people thought. "The soldiers ate with the queen!" They went to get their milk from the wells. The soldiers stirred the milk into the hot soup as the people looked on. At last the soup was done.

"The soup is ready," the soldiers said, "but to eat stone soup we all need to sit together. We need a big, long table."

The people put many tables together. They made a huge table in the middle of the village. One man asked, "Don't we need bread and something to drink with this fine soup?"

Soon all kinds of food were spread on the table and everyone sat down to eat. Imagine eating a soup made from stones!

Never before had the people been so happy. Never before had there been such fun. The people ate and ate. After that, they danced late into the night.

Then the first soldier asked, "Is there a bed of straw where we could sleep?"

"We wouldn't think of letting you sleep on straw," the people said.

So the soldiers got to sleep in the longest, finest beds in the village.

"Many thanks for what you showed us," said a man the next morning. "We will never go hungry, now that we know how to make stone soup."

"Just remember," said the first soldier, "you begin with three smooth stones." Then the soldiers went on their way.

Meet the Author

Nancy Ross Ryan likes to write for children. She thinks "Stone Soup" has something special to say about being friends. "The soldiers were hungry and cold, but they knew how to share. Only they could teach the people about sharing," she said.

LOOKING BACK

Thinking About the Section

You read about Gina and Grandpa and the new friend they made. You read about two animal friends, Duck and Bear. Then you read about three soldiers who made friends with the people in a village.

Writing About the Section

Think about what the people and animals did for their friends. On your own paper, write five sentences that tell what one friend did for the other. Start your sentences with the words you see.

1. Gina caught
2. The woman gave Gina and Grandpa
3. Duck gave Bear
4. Bear gave Duck
5. The soldiers helped the people

Books to Read

The Sun's Asleep Behind the Hill
by Mirra Ginsburg

Read what happens when the day changes into night. Find out what some animals and people do when the sky gets dark. This book uses a song and pictures to tell what happens.

Max by Rachel Isadora

Max uses his hands as he plays on a ball team. Read about one more way Max gets exercise. Find out what he learns to like.

Burton and Dudley
by Marjorie Weinman Sharmat

Burton and Dudley are two opossums who are very good friends. Find out what they do for each other. You may laugh at the funny things they do.

Mom...

may I
keep it?

4

Time to Laugh

What makes you laugh? You may laugh when you hear a funny joke or see a cartoon. You may laugh when something funny happens.

Look through pages 138–177 and find out what funny things and people you will read about. Look for pictures of things that make you laugh.

Finding What It's All About

Look at the picture. If someone asks you what the picture is all about, you would say it is about animals. It looks funny. You can see that the picture is not about people or places.

When you read, you need to know what a story or article is all about. In just one or two words you could tell someone what you have been reading about. As you read, you may find clues that help you. Each sentence may tell you about one thing. You may read one word many times in the sentences. Pictures may help you too.

Read the sentences to find out what they are all about. See what each sentence tells.

A play is a story told by people. They may be in costumes. To put on a play, the people practice their lines many times. Then they practice with each other on a stage. They like the audience to laugh.

1. What are the sentences all about? How can you tell?

If you said the sentences are all about a play, you were right. You know because each sentence tells something about a play.

Puppets make us laugh. The people who work the puppets tell a funny story. They make the puppets talk and move. The audience laughs at the puppets.

2. What are the sentences all about? How can you tell?

The sentences are about puppets. Every sentence tells about puppets. The picture helps you too.

Some people write books to make others laugh. The books have funny pictures and tell funny things that happen. Reading a funny book is fun.

3. What are the sentences all about? Answer in one or two words.

Practicing to Find What It's All About
Read the sentences to find out what they are all about.

Cartoons are pictures that can tell a story. In cartoons, animals can talk. The animals and people in cartoons may look funny and do funny things.

1. What are the sentences all about?
2. How do you know?

Tips for Reading on Your Own
- Ask what the next selection, "Pictures for Fun" is all about. Answer in one or two words.
- Ask if your answer fits what you read.

Pictures for Fun

by Ruth Kaye

A cartoon is a drawing that tells a story or a joke on paper. It may make people laugh. Carol Lea Benjamin draws cartoons because she likes to make children laugh.

When Ms. Benjamin gets ready to draw a cartoon, all she needs are a piece of paper and a pencil. She needs to be able to draw a circle too. Then she can draw cartoons.

To make a rabbit, Ms. Benjamin draws a circle for its head. Next she draws two big ears. Inside the circle, Ms. Benjamin adds two tiny lines for eyes. Then she draws a tiny circle for a nose. Last she adds a mouth. She draws other animals by starting the same way.

When Ms. Benjamin draws people's faces, she starts with circles again. She adds eyes, ears, noses, and mouths. She adds hair so the faces look funny.

To make cartoons, Ms. Benjamin practices drawing different kinds of noses, ears, and hands. She draws a page of noses, a page of ears, and a page of hands. Then she uses the drawings in her cartoons.

I wonder if I'll get a bike for my BIRTHDAY, which is next TUESDAY...

Ms. Benjamin shows how people and animals feel by the way she draws their faces. The boy in one drawing wishes for a bike next Tuesday. He looks afraid to say it. Tuesday is special, because Tuesday is his birthday.

To change the way someone in a cartoon feels, Ms. Benjamin moves or changes the lines on the face.

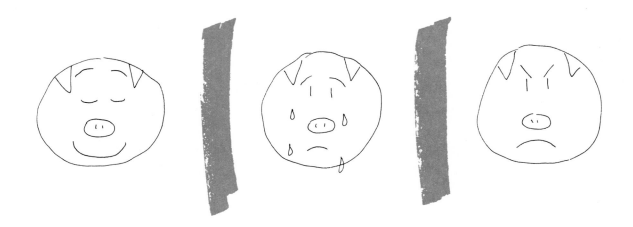

Before Ms. Benjamin draws animals and people, she looks at real pictures of them. Then she draws them doing something funny. Sometimes Ms. Benjamin draws animals that do what people do. She may draw a cartoon of a story she once read. She changes the story to make her cartoon funny.

Ms. Benjamin keeps a list of funny things she sees. Then, when she is ready to draw, she picks something from her list. She thinks of all the ways it could be funny. Ms. Benjamin may draw a porcupine with a nice pine tree for a friend. Or she may draw a huge giant with a very tiny pet.

Ms. Benjamin began drawing cartoons when she started writing books for children. She liked dogs so much that she learned to be a dog trainer. Then she wrote books about training dogs. Ms. Benjamin made cartoon drawings of dogs for the books.

Once someone told Ms. Benjamin that her cartoons were good, she began drawing more. She wrote a book about cartooning. She thought it would be fun for children to be able to draw their own cartoons.

Ms. Benjamin likes her work. She likes writing and cartooning for children.

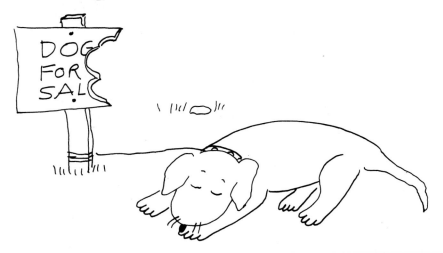

MAKING PEOPLE LAUGH

by Thelma Gruenbaum

Bill Cosby is a very special, funny man. His job is to make people laugh. He likes making people laugh. He likes helping them learn too. Bill Cosby teaches people about each other through his jokes.

Bill Cosby is always busy. Sometimes he is busy telling jokes to an audience or working on his TV and cartoon shows. He writes some of the TV shows he is in. Work keeps Bill Cosby very busy.

Sometimes Bill Cosby is on TV shows that teach children to read. He thinks that everyone needs to be able to read. During the shows, Bill Cosby helps children learn to read. He does funny things or sings and dances. He makes learning to read fun.

Bill Cosby helps us laugh at the things we do. During one show, he tells about a funny shirt that he got from his children. First he shows the audience the shirt. The shirt has big colored flowers all over it. Then Bill Cosby puts on a funny tie that his children once gave him for his birthday.

Bill Cosby puts a funny hat on his head.
The hat has many lights on it. The lights
shine in the dark. How funny he looks!
When he is ready, Bill Cosby turns the lights
on. He thanks his children for the nice things
they give him, but says a kiss would be just
as nice. The whole audience laughs.

Bill Cosby is able to make people of any
age laugh. When he tells a joke, he may use
his voice and his whole face. He opens his
eyes wide, moves his nose, or changes
his voice.

People learn from Bill Cosby's TV and cartoon shows. People see that what happens to them happens to others too. Bill Cosby's jokes are funny because people know how it feels to have the same thing happen to them.

Bill Cosby talks about the feelings people share. During his show, he may talk about hearing a noise at night. He knows that everyone has been afraid of the dark before. Bill Cosby can tell a joke about it and make the whole audience laugh.

Bill Cosby likes to make people laugh. He likes the kind of work he does.

Meet a Reader

Michelle Cobb is 7 years old. She lives in Colorado.

"Reading is fun," says Michelle. "Books help me learn about new things. I like books about animals and books that are funny. Amelia Bedelia is a book I like to read again and again, because it makes me laugh."

Michelle likes to read to her family, but she still likes it when her mom or dad reads to her. Everyone in Michelle's family likes to hear a story.

Checking Comprehension and Skills

Thinking About What You've Read

- **1.** Who is "Pictures for Fun" all about?
    - a. someone who sings
    - b. someone who draws cartoons
    - c. someone on TV
- **2.** What is funny about the last cartoon on page 144?
- **3.** Who is "Making People Laugh" all about?
- **4.** Would you want to have a job like Bill Cosby's? Why or why not?
- **5.** How do you know that Ms. Benjamin and Mr. Cosby like children?

Talking About What You've Read

Carol Lea Benjamin and Bill Cosby make people laugh. Tell about something funny that has made you laugh this week.

Writing About What You've Read

Write a story about something funny that made you laugh. Draw a cartoon to go with your story.

- Comprehension: Main idea

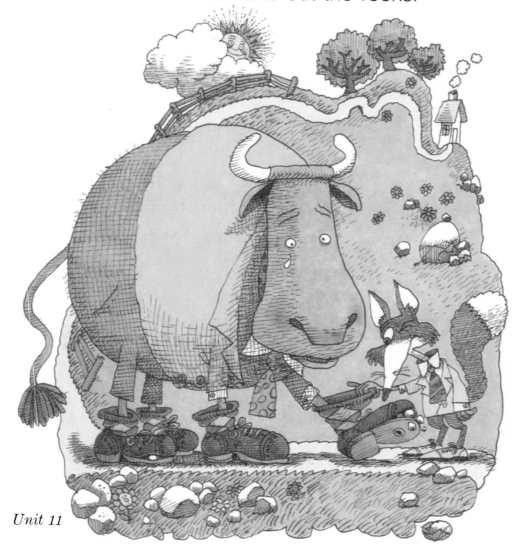

"THERE ARE ROCKS," IN MY SOCKS! SAID THE OX TO THE FOX

by
Patricia
Thomas

PART 1: "There are rocks in my socks,"
Said the ox to the fox.
"Bumpy old, bumpy old,
Bumpy old rocks.
I feel very grumpy
With rocks in my socks!"

PART 2: "See here, my fine friend,"
Said the fox to the ox.
"Stop being so grumpy
And take out the rocks.

"I must say I know,
   That the longer one talks
   The less time one has
   For taking out rocks."

PART 1: "But there isn't a way,"
   Said the ox to the fox,
"To get rid of the rocks
   That are inside my socks.
   With my shoes just under,
   My feet right on top,
   I see no way at all to
   Get rid of the rocks."

PART 2:   Said the fox to the ox,
            "There MUST be a way
            To get rocks out of socks.
            I know! I have it!
            Just do a flip flop,
            Put your legs in the air,
            With your feet off the top
            Of the rocks, which will then
            Slide right out of your socks."

PART 1: "Oh my, you are clever,"
            Said the ox to the fox.
            "I will do a flip flop,
            With my feet not on top,
            So the rocks will come falling
            Right out of my socks!"

ALL: Flip . . . Flop . . . But nothing
            falls out!

PART 3: Said a bird to the ox,
"Just take off your shoes
Then take off your socks
Try holding your nose
As you let out the rocks.
Next, put back each sock
And put back each shoe . . .
Which is all, Mr. Ox,
That you needed to do."

PART 1: "All I needed to do
To get rid of the rocks
Was to take off my shoes
And tip over my socks?"

PART 3: "Why, yes," said the bird.

ALL: Giggle . . . Giggle . . .
Fall, fall, fall!

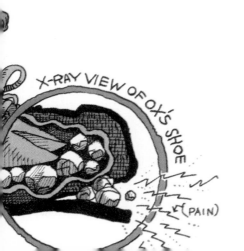

X-RAY VIEW OF OX'S SHOE
(PAIN)

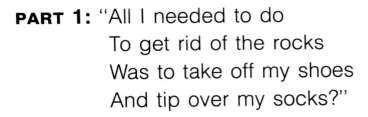

The Golden Goose

a play from the story by the Brothers Grimm

THE PLAYERS

FATHER

MOTHER

HANS

CLEVER TOM

CLEVER JOHN

MAN

PRINCESS

KING

SISTER 1

SISTER 2

STORYTELLER: Once there was a man who had three sons. His oldest son was Clever John and his middle son, Clever Tom. His last son was Hans. People always made fun of Hans, because they thought he was less clever than his brothers.

CLEVER JOHN: Father, may Tom and I go to saw some wood today?

FATHER: Yes, you may go. We need some wood for the cold days coming soon.

MOTHER: Take some good cake to eat when you get hungry. You'll need water too.

CLEVER TOM: Thank you, Mother.

STORYTELLER: The two older sons walked to the woods. Next to a tree, they saw a man. He was sitting on a gray stone.

MAN: Could I help you get rid of some of that cake and water? I am very hungry.

CLEVER JOHN: If we share our food with you, there will be less for us to eat.

CLEVER TOM: Be off with you! We have nothing to give you. (MAN *walks away.)*

STORYTELLER: The brothers began to saw down a tree. As they did, their saws fell into pieces. The brothers could cut no more, so they went home.

HANS: Father, please may I go to saw wood?

FATHER: Your brothers came home without any wood. I don't think you can do better.

MOTHER: If you must go, take some old bread and water with you.

STORYTELLER: Hans went into the woods. He saw the same man, sitting on a stone.

MAN: Please share your bread and water with me so that I will not go hungry.

HANS: Take all the food you need.

STORYTELLER: When Hans took out the old bread, it turned into the finest of cakes. The two sat and ate together.

MAN: Thank you, Hans. You have been very kind. I want to do something nice for you. Next to that stone stands a tree. Saw it down and you will find something special. (MAN *walks away.*)

STORYTELLER: Hans sawed away at the tree. All at once, a golden goose flew into the air. Hans wanted to hold the fine bird, so he reached up into the air to get it. Hans started for home, holding the goose as he walked. On the way, two sisters stopped him.

SISTER 1: Let me touch the goose. I want one of its golden feathers. *(She touches the goose.)* Oh no, my hand is stuck!

SISTER 2: I want a golden feather too. *(She touches her sister.)* Help! I am stuck!

STORYTELLER: A bit later, Hans's brothers came looking for him. They saw Hans, the goose, and two sisters. The brothers reached out with their hands, so they, too, stuck to the others.

STORYTELLER: Hans walked on until he reached a little village. There he saw a princess, looking sad and grumpy.

KING: Nobody makes the princess laugh. Dancers and singers can't make her smile. The one who makes her laugh will be the new prince.

HANS: I can! *(HANS runs past the princess.)*

PRINCESS *(starting to giggle)*: Look at that boy holding a golden goose! And look at all the people stuck to him! What a funny thing to see! *(She giggles.)*

KING *(to HANS)*: How clever of you, new prince! You made the princess laugh.

STORYTELLER: And during his years as the prince, no one made fun of Hans again.

Checking Comprehension and Skills

Thinking About What You've Read

- **1.** What does the ox do to get rid of the rocks in his socks?
- **2.** Why do you think the ox may like the bird?
- **3.** In "The Golden Goose," what makes the princess laugh?
- **4.** Why do people follow Hans?
- **5.** How would the story be different if the goose had not been golden?
- **6.** What makes you laugh?

Talking About What You've Read

Imagine you are the fox. Tell what funny way you could get rid of the ox's rocks. Then imagine you are Hans and tell what funny things happen to you when you find a golden goose.

Writing About What You've Read

Write about what you would do if you were Hans and someone gave you a golden goose. Tell about people following you.

- Comprehension: Cause and effect relationships

Learning About Blends

straw

strike

You know that words like *swim, float,* and *grin* begin with two consonants that stand for the sound of the letters blended together. Some words begin with three consonants that stand for the sound of the letters blended together.

Look at the picture of the ship. Listen as you say the words in the ship that begin alike. *Straw* and *strike* begin with the consonant letters *s, t, r.* The letters stand for the sound of the consonants blended together, the str sound.

Look at the pictures and say the words on the next page.

 splits

 screen

Good. Now say the word or words in each box. Remember to blend the sound of the three consonant letters at the beginning.

stripe	splits	screen
strike		scrub
strap		scrape

Practicing with Blends

Read the sentences to find out what is funny. The words you read must make sense.

1. A big fish flops its tail in the water and makes a big, wet *splash*.
2. People are so afraid, they *scream*.
3. Clever Sal can hold the fish in the air because she is so *strong*.

Tips for Reading on Your Own

- If a word begins with three consonants, blend the sound of the letters together.
- Your word must make sense in the sentence.

Stormalong
the Sailor

as told by Mary Hynes-Berry

"Look at the clouds," said Sailor Sam to a new sailor named Dan. "See how the wind is blowing? I wonder if a storm is coming. It might be a Stormalong Day."

"What is a Stormalong Day?" asked Dan.

"A Stormalong Day is the kind of cold, wet day Stormalong likes," said Sam. "You must not know about Stormalong the Sailor. Well, get ready to listen to my story."

As a baby, Stormalong was so big that the only bed big enough to hold him was a boat down by the sea. Well, one night, after his mother put him to bed, Stormalong started to swing his feet up and down. The boat began rocking. A small wave began to splash over some stones. The people in the town by the sea could hear the splashing.

Stormalong moved his feet faster. The small waves got bigger. The people wondered what might happen next.

One wave was so big, it splashed out the light in the lighthouse. That light was Stormalong's night light! The baby did not scream or cry. He did what he should have done. He stopped swinging his feet. The boat stopped rocking. Waves stopped splashing. But the lighthouse stayed dark.

Stormalong had to do something fast! He reached up into the sky. He took one small star to put inside the lighthouse. Once again Stormalong had a night light.

Stormalong never was a small baby. So as a boy, he got bigger and bigger. Some people say he was one of the biggest boys in America. Stormalong got so big, his head touched the sky.

Stormalong was strong too. Once he and his friends saw a shark swimming in the water next to the village. Stormalong thought he might be strong enough to help the shark. It was swimming in circles, looking for a way back to the deep sea.

Stormalong's friends wondered what they should do for the shark. They talked to each other about how to help the shark. They saw it zigzag this way and that. Stormalong did not stop to talk with his friends. He did not wonder what he should do. He went to help the shark all by himself.

Stormalong was so strong, he was able to pick up the shark. He got ready to throw it across the water to its home in the sea. With one great throw, the shark was back in deep water swimming home.

Sailor Sam went on to say, "Stormalong did grow up to sail his own ship. He sailed across the sea and back home to America."

Once Stormalong saw a huge octopus. The grumpy thing put an arm around the ship to hold it. The ship zigzagged to a stop.

Stormalong did not scream or get mad. He just smiled and said in a very nice voice, "Do you think you might let go, please?"

The octopus would not let go of the ship. It reached up with a different arm. It took Stormalong's cap to throw it away.

Now Stormalong was not happy about that. "You should not stop my ship," Stormalong said to the octopus. "And you should NEVER throw away my cap," he shouted.

Stormalong was a good swimmer, so he jumped into the sea after the octopus. First Stormalong took his cap back. Next he pulled each arm of the octopus away from the ship. The ship began to zigzag as water splashed here and there. At last, the strong octopus left the ship and went swimming away.

Once Stormalong saw that the octopus could stop his ship, he wondered if he should get a bigger ship. He thought the one he had might be too small. So he got the biggest ship he was able to find.

Stormalong sailed on with his huge new ship. It was taking soap across the sea to America. The ship had to sail through the water with close, dark cliffs on both sides.

Smaller ships could sail right by the cliffs, but not this one. Stormalong's huge ship touched the cliffs on both sides.

"Oh no," said a sailor on the ship. "We might have to sail the long way to America."

"No!" said Stormalong. "Get out all the soap inside. We will paint the sides of the ship with it. We will just have to slide past the cliffs."

The sailors wondered how the soap would help as they got busy painting the ship.

The ship started moving. Because of the soap, the ship was able to slide right by the cliffs. The soap had made the sides of the ship smooth.

As the ship moved, the white soap came off the sides of the ship. The soap stuck to the dark cliffs. They had turned from dark to white. To this day, you can still see where Stormalong's ship passed by the cliffs. The cliffs are still white.

"Well, Dan," said Sailor Sam. "Now you know everything about Stormalong the Sailor and the places he has been and things he has done. That is enough for now. After all, you and I should get busy. We have some sailing of our own to do!"

Checking Comprehension and Skills

Thinking About What You've Read
1. What is Stormalong like?
• 2. What does Stormalong do to get the night light working?
3. Why do you think the octopus stops the ship?
• 4. How do the sailors use the soap on Stormalong's ship?
5. Which part of the story would be fun to tell?

Talking About What You've Read
Imagine you are Stormalong. Think about what happens to you in the story. Tell a part of the story as if you are Stormalong.

Writing About What You've Read
Think of something that could happen to you as Stormalong. Write some sentences to tell what you would do.

• Comprehension: Details

Fish Song

by Margaret Wise Brown

Oh the lobster and the fish
And the fish and the whale,
You can't catch a fish
With an old tin pail
And you can't catch a lobster
With a hook and a line
And you can't catch a whale at all.

Catch a lobster in a pot
And a fish on a line
Fish in the nets
When the weather is fine
But if you ever try to catch a whale,
He will knock you down flat
With a flip of his tail.

LOOKING BACK

Thinking About the Section

You have read about people who have jobs to make others laugh. You read about some funny things that happen with an ox and a golden goose. Last you read about the sailor, Stormalong, who does funny things.

See if you can tell how the people and animals make others laugh. On your own paper, write how each does something funny.

Who or What?	How are they funny?
Bill Cosby	says funny things
Carol Benjamin	
Ox	
Fox	
The boy, the goose, and the people	
Stormalong	

Writing About the Section

Write two or more sentences about a person or animal you liked best in this section.

5

Birds

There are many kinds of birds. They have different shapes, feathers, and colors. Some birds fly, but others can't. Birds may build nests for their baby birds. People enjoy feeding and listening to birds.

Look through pages 180–216 to find out what birds you'll read about. See how the birds are different from each other.

Learning About Goal and Outcome

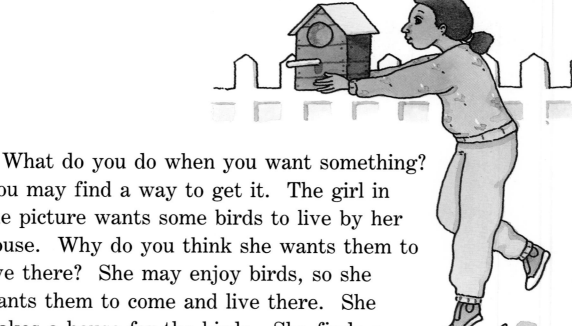

What do you do when you want something? You may find a way to get it. The girl in the picture wants some birds to live by her house. Why do you think she wants them to live there? She may enjoy birds, so she wants them to come and live there. She makes a house for the birds. She finds a way to get what she wants.

The characters in a story may want something. They try to get what they want. When you read a story, you can find out why the characters want something and what they do to get it. After reading, you'll know if the characters get what they want.

Read to find out what Carlos wants and if he gets what he wants.

In the spring, Carlos looks for birds that fly around his home. Carlos wants a book of his own about birds. Then he can find out which kinds of birds he sees. He will keep track of the kinds of birds he sees. After school each day, Carlos works doing jobs for the man next door. Soon Carlos is able to buy the book he wants.

1. What does Carlos want?

The second sentence tells you that Carlos wants a book of his own.

2. Why does Carlos want it?

The third sentence tells you that Carlos will keep track of the birds he sees. You know that the book will help Carlos do that.

3. What does Carlos do to get what he wants? Read the sentence that tells what Carlos does for the man next door.
4. Does Carlos get what he wants? Read the last sentence for the answer.

Practicing Goal and Outcome

Read the paragraph to find out what Lynn wants. Then see if she gets what she wants.

In the spring, Lynn likes to see birds make their nests. She wants to get a bird to make its nest outside her house. Lynn puts an old shoelace, tiny pieces of rope, and some rocks on a table outside. Days later, only the rocks are left. She sees her shoelace and the rope pieces in a bird's nest in the tree.

1. What does Lynn want?
2. Does Lynn get what she wants? If she does, what does she do to get it?

Tips for Reading on Your Own

- In the next story, "The Magpie's Nest," think about what the characters want.
- Ask what the characters do to get what they want.
- Ask if the characters get what they want.

The Magpie's Nest

an English folk tale

One day all the birds of the air came to see Madge Magpie. They asked her to teach them how to build a nest, for the magpie is the cleverest bird of all at building nests.

Madge Magpie began to show the birds how to build a nest. First of all, she took some mud and made a kind of round cake with it.

The thrush said, "Oh, that is how it is done." Away the thrush flew. That is why thrushes build their round nests with mud.

The turtledove was not listening to Madge Magpie. In a soft voice she said, "Take two, Taffy, take two." This was the turtledove's call.

The magpie went on. She brought some twigs to the nest. She spread the twigs around in the mud. The blackbird looked on.

"Now I know all about it," said the blackbird. Off he flew to make a nest of mud and twigs. That is how blackbirds make their nests to this very day.

Madge Magpie was not finished. She put more mud over the twigs.

"Oh, I already know that," said the wise owl. The owl flew away to build his own nest. To this day, owls can't make good nests.

Still the turtledove would not listen. She said again, "Take two, Taffy, take two."

Madge Magpie did not hear the turtledove. She started weaving some twigs around the nest. Then she brought some feathers and lined the round nest with them.

"That is fine for me," said the starling. Then the starling flew away to begin its nest. Now starlings enjoy nice, soft nests.

So it went on. Every bird learned a bit about building nests. Not one bird stayed to watch Madge finish except the turtledove, who had only said, "Take two, Taffy, take two," the whole time.

Madge Magpie had worked without looking up. She did not know that all the birds behind her had left except the turtledove. When she did hear the turtledove say, "Take two," Madge was putting a twig across the nest. "One more twig is enough," said Madge.

Then she saw no one was left except the turtledove. Madge flew away and never wanted to teach the birds again. That is why different birds build different kinds of nests.

Goose Feathers

by Emma L. Brock

Things always happened to Debby and Tim. It was that way with the goose feathers that Mrs. Wiggin had put in the feather house.

"The new teacher is coming here to live," said Mrs. Wiggin. "We must make some new pillows for her bed."

The three went into the feather house and closed the door. Many soft, white feathers were on the table.

Mrs. Wiggin said, "Here are the bags for the pillows. We will stuff them with feathers."

Mrs. Wiggin put some feathers into a bag that Tim brought for her. Debby clapped her hands to make the feathers fly about. When she giggled, a cloud of them would float up. The feathers sailed up and then floated down again to the table.

"Oh, the baby is crying," said Mrs. Wiggin. "I was wishing she would sleep until we finished. I'll have to take her and feed her. You hold this, Debby. Tim can put the feathers in. I'll be back soon. If you go out, remember to close the door behind you."

"Yes," said Tim.

Tim stuffed the feathers in. "Hold the
bag wide open," he said to his sister.

"Oh!" screamed Debby. "There's a feather
on my nose. It feels funny. Take it off."

"Blow it off," said Tim, "and hold still.
You are stirring up all the feathers."

Debby jumped and waved the pillow over
her head. Feathers floated about the feather
house, looking like snow.

"Stop it, stop it!" shouted Tim. He was
running behind Debby trying to catch her.
She screamed and pulled away. She opened
the door and ran out.

Tim ran out of the feather house after
Debby. The two ran into the field. In the
middle of the field Tim caught her from
behind. He said, "Give me that pillow."

The pillow flew up in the air. Out of it
floated a cloud of feathers. A strong wind
blew. Off went the feathers into the woods.
Debby watched them. "There go some of the
teacher's feathers," she said, pointing.

"Tim! Debby!" their mother called. She
pointed as she ran to the feather house.

Tim and Debby ran across the field as
fast as they could.

Feathers floated like snow into the apple trees. Tim had left the door open!

All three looked into the feather house. There were only about six feathers left. The three watched the other feathers blow past the trees. Mrs. Wiggin pointed to the trees and said, "There go two good pillows."

Tim said nothing. And Debby said nothing. The feathers flew around all day. When Mr. Wiggin came back from the woods, he had feathers in his hair.

Only the birds were happy. They were singing and picking up feathers to line their nests. All the birds had soft feather beds to enjoy that year. But there were no new pillows for the new teacher's bed.

Checking Comprehension and Skills

Thinking About What You've Read

- **1.** In "The Magpie's Nest," what do the thrush, owl, blackbird, and starling want? Do they get what they want?

  2. In "The Magpie's Nest," what did the birds do that real birds can't do?

  3. Why do you think there are different kinds of bird nests?

- **4.** In "Goose Feathers," what does Mrs. Wiggin want? Does she get it?

  5. Imagine you are Tim or Debby. How would you feel if you saw the feathers outside?

Talking About What You've Read

Imagine you are a bird in "Goose Feathers." Tell what happens one day when you are flying by the feather house.

Writing About What You've Read

You are still the bird by the feather house. Write what you do when you see all the feathers. Tell what they look like.

- Literary Skill: Goal and outcome

Sing, Mockingbird

by Charnan Simon

Little Feather's real name was Little-Sister-to-Our-Many-Feathered-Friends. That was too long a name for such a little girl, so the Indians in her village just called her Little Feather.

Little Feather had been a friend to the birds as long as she could remember. The owl, the magpie, the starling—she knew them all. This was just as it should be, for didn't the old stories all say it was the children who should care for the birds?

Little Feather remembered what the storyteller had said about the birds. It was long ago, when she was just a tiny girl. She and her friends sat under a cold winter moon. Far into the night they listened to the old storyteller weave his words.

"In the old days this was said," began the storyteller. "Birds were made from leaves that fell from the trees when summer was over. Their feathers took on the colors of the falling leaves. Many were a rich brown. Some were bright red or yellow. Others were warm orange, and some special ones were golden. You can still see all the colors of the earth in the wing of a bird."

The storyteller smiled at the circle of listening children. "Birds are like leaves in other ways, too. Have you ever watched leaves falling from the trees? They float in the air before they touch the ground. Birds can float in the air, too. They can fly high and low. They belong both to earth and to sky."

The storyteller went on. "Like the leaves, many birds go away when the cold winter winds blow. But when the new little green leaves grow out in spring, the birds come back."

"Then the birds make their homes in the trees. The birds know they are safe among the leaves. Some birds build their nests in the grass, but they perch high in the trees during the day. They like to be as close to the leaves as they can."

Little Feather remembered the storyteller saying, "The birds are our friends. They are the special friends of children. They sing sweet songs to wake you in the morning. In the nighttime their soft sounds help you sleep. As the birds care for you, you must care for the birds."

All this Little Feather was told when she was a very little girl. Some of her friends did not remember the story as they grew older, but Little Feather always did. She always remembered. The birds were her special friends.

Winter was fine for telling stories, but Little Feather liked it better when summer came. Then all her bird friends flew back from their winter homes. The village was loud with bird calls.

"Hello, Brother Blackbird," Little Feather would call out. "I see your wife is busy building your nest. Why won't you help her?"

Sometimes Little Feather would watch Sister Woodpecker climb right up the side of a tree. The bird was looking for a hole to build her nest.

"I wish I could climb like that," Little Feather would say.

At other times, Little Feather helped her friends find food. "Over here, Brother Redbird! Look under this rock. There are many insects here. They will help your babies grow big and strong." Little Feather watched the redbird take the insects in his beak and feed them to his young family. The baby birds were always so hungry!

One fine morning Little Feather was giving her friends some berries to eat. Many of the birds came so near, they ate right out of her fingers. Some stayed back a little. Others stayed farther away, but they got berries too.

Little Feather's mother came over to watch. "What fine friends you have," she said. "Can you tell me all their names?"

"Oh, yes," said Little Feather. "This is Sister Thrush. Don't her orange feathers look warm and soft? Over there is Brother Woodpecker. He has a fine black and white jacket, but his cap is bright red! See how long his beak is. He can tap, tap, tap right through the trees with that beak!"

A bird with bright red feathers hopped up to Little Feather and her mother. "You can't miss Brother Redbird," said Little Feather. "All his feathers are red. See how they shine! And look—there is Sister Canary. She is the finest of all, with her golden wings."

Little Feather's mother smiled. "Who is your little gray friend?" she asked. She pointed to a small bird hopping on the ground.

Little Feather frowned. "Oh, that is only Sister Mockingbird."

"What? Don't you like Sister Mockingbird?" asked her mother. She seemed angry.

"She is all right," said Little Feather, "but the other birds are so pretty. Sister Mockingbird's feathers are the color of the sky when it rains. She is nobody special."

Now it was Little Feather's mother who frowned. "Do birds need pretty feathers to be special?" she asked. "Sister Mockingbird can sound like every other bird, and her own song is the sweetest of all. Of all the birds, she alone sings to make her listeners happy. This makes her a very special bird!"

Little Feather thought about what her mother had said. "Still," she answered, "it is too bad that she isn't prettier!"

So the summer passed. Little Feather and her friends were busy and happy. Then, all too soon, the days grew colder. Winter was coming. It wouldn't be long before the birds flew off to their winter homes.

When Little Feather woke up one morning, she couldn't get out of bed. Her face felt hot. Her head hurt. She couldn't move her arms and legs. She was afraid.

The days passed, and Little Feather did not get any better. Even the wise woman of the village could not help her.

Winter came. The sky turned gray, and the winds blew cold. Snow fell soft and deep in the village. Little Feather thought she would never see summer again.

"If only I could smell the flowers," Little Feather cried. "Or feel a soft summer rain! I wish so much that I could hear my sweet birds sing. I know I could get well then!"

The birds could not come to Little Feather. Many were already in their winter homes, far from the village. The ones that were left were busy finding food for the cold winter. They did not have time to sing.

Then one night, when the soft light of the moon was shining outside, Little Feather did hear a sound. A bird song! It sounded as if Brother Blackbird had come to pay a visit! After him, Sister Thrush sang her sweetest song. Then came the starling, the turtle dove, and the magpie. Even Brother Owl added his low call. Little Feather could hear all of her old friends.

So it went. All through that cold winter night, the sweet birds sang for Little Feather. When the sun got up from its bed the next morning, Little Feather left hers, too.

"I am well!" said the happy girl. "Now I must thank my friends, for it was their singing that made me better!"

When Little Feather looked outside, what did she see? One small gray bird, hopping in the snow. It was the mockingbird. Of all the birds, only she had answered Little Feather's cry.

"Sweet singer, I am sorry," said Little Feather. "I once said you were nobody special, but you came when I needed you. You sang for all the other birds who could not be here. It was your singing that made me well. How can I thank you?"

Sister Mockingbird did not want thanks. She just wanted to sing, and she did. She opened her beak wide, and she sang, and she sang, and she sang.

Meet the Illustrator

Helen Nelson Reed has always liked to draw. She used to draw her own pictures next to the pictures in the books she read. She likes birds, and used to feed them when she was little. She likes to draw bird wings because they make people think of things that move.

Checking Comprehension and Skills

Thinking About What You've Read
1. How does the mockingbird help Little Feather during the winter?
• 2. How does Little Feather feel about the mockingbird before she gets sick?
3. Why does Little Feather's mother say the mockingbird is special?
• 4. How does Little Feather feel about the mockingbird when she gets well?
5. If you were Little Feather, how would you show your thanks to the mockingbird?

Talking About What You've Read
   Imagine you are the mockingbird. Tell how you feel about Little Feather not liking you as much as the other birds. Then tell how you feel when Little Feather gets sick.

Writing About What You've Read
   If you were the mockingbird, would you help Little Feather get better? Write a sentence telling why you feel as you do.

• Literary Skill: Character

Birds Through the Year

by Mary Hynes-Berry

In the Fall

In the fall, in some places, the leaves on the trees change colors. The sun sets sooner each day. The days are still warm, but people know <u>winter</u> is coming. They start thinking about winter. Some birds get ready for winter too.

Winter in the <u>North</u> may be too cold for some birds. There will be <u>fewer</u> hours of daylight and little food to eat. No flowers or fruits will grow. There will be fewer insects to eat. So the birds get ready to fly <u>south</u>.

During the warm weeks of fall, the birds
eat and eat. They must be strong enough to
fly far away. They will fly south to warm
places for the winter.

Birds such as **ducks** and **thrushes** fly a
long way to warm places. The tiny
hummingbird heads south for the winter too.

Some birds of the North can live through
the cold winter. If you look outside, maybe
you will see either a **woodpecker** or a
chickadee looking for food. The birds find
dry berries and seeds to eat. Their feathers
keep them warm when it is cold.

Flying South

When birds fly south, they need to know which way to go. Birds either fly together in a flock or all alone. When birds fly in a flock, one bird shows the other birds the way. If you look into the sky in the fall, you may see birds flying in a flock.

Some birds fly alone. By looking at where the sun, moon, and stars are in the sky, they can tell where they are. As they fly alone, they call out to other birds like them. Then they listen for the calls of other birds so they know where to find food. The birds find their way to food and a warm winter place by helping each other.

In the Spring

When spring comes, the days get warm once again. The sun stays out longer in the day. Flowers and plants start growing. There are many insects and fruits for birds to eat. The birds hurry north again to places they left months ago.

Once they are back, the birds build nests for their eggs. The eggs hatch. The baby birds learn to fly. They eat to grow bigger and stronger. Then, in the fall, the little birds will be ready to make their first long trip south for the winter.

Baby birds hatched each spring by one mother

🥚 = 1 baby bird

Water Thrush	🥚 🥚 🥚 🥚 🥚
Wood Duck	🥚 🥚 🥚 🥚 🥚 🥚 🥚 🥚 🥚 🥚
Redwing Blackbird	🥚 🥚 🥚 🥚
Woodpecker	🥚 🥚 🥚 🥚 🥚
Hummingbird	🥚 🥚

Bird in a Hurry

by Joanne Bernstein

This special bird is smaller than any other bird. It flies very fast. Its feathers are bright and they shine in the sun's light. This bird makes a buzzing sound when it flies. What kind of bird is it? Maybe you already know. It's a hummingbird, a bird that does flying tricks in the air.

Long ago, hummingbirds got their name because of the sound their wings made when they flew. They make this sound because they move their wings very fast. Hummingbirds are not shy birds, but they are hard to see. If you see a hummingbird in North America, you may see its bright, green feathers. It may have either a red throat or a white throat. Its throat color tells which kind of hummingbird it is.

Bird Sizes

	![bar] = 1 inch
Hummingbird	▯▯▯
Starling	▯▯▯▯▯▯▯▯
Blackbird	▯▯▯▯▯▯▯▯▯
Chickadee	▯▯▯▯▯
Woodpecker	▯▯▯▯▯▯▯▯▯▯

Some hummingbirds are only as big as your finger. They are small enough to hold in your hand. You could never catch a hummingbird, because it does not stay in one place long enough! Hummingbirds are not shy, but always in a hurry.

Hummingbirds like the color red. To feed hummingbirds, people put honey in colored red water so it will taste sweet. They put the water in a feeder outside a window. Then the people watch for the little flyers to come and taste the sweet water. As hummingbirds eat, they keep moving their wings. Then they hurry away.

Hummingbirds eat many, many times every day. The food helps them to be strong flyers. Hummingbirds reach deep inside flowers with their long beaks. They like the sweet taste they find. Hummingbirds eat insects too. Sometimes the birds find bugs inside the flowers.

Hummingbirds are small, but they are not shy or afraid. When bigger birds follow them, they turn around and fly after them. Other birds leave hummingbirds alone because they are afraid of the hummingbird's long beak. The tiny hummingbird flies faster than a bee.

Maybe you've seen a hummingbird fly. It can do more flying tricks than any other bird. When a hummingbird flies, it can move up and down. It can fly backward too. It is the only bird that can fly backward or stay in one place. The hummingbird zigzags here and there, flips over, and then flies backward.

The hummingbird never walks, because it can't walk. Its legs and feet are very small, and are not strong enough to walk on. Because a hummingbird's wings are so strong, it flies when it moves to something close.

Before winter comes, the hummingbirds that live in North America begin to eat and eat. They get ready to leave the North. Then, the hummingbirds fly south. For many nights, they fly far to reach their winter homes. Each night they fly without stopping to eat or sleep. At last the birds reach the place where they will stay all winter.

In the spring, the tiny hummingbirds fly north. The flipping, flying, zigzagging hummingbirds go back where they lived months ago. They build their nests from plants and leaves. Later, the little baby birds begin learning hummingbird tricks. They, too, will be birds in a hurry.

Checking Comprehension and Skills

Thinking About What You've Read

1. Why do birds fly south for the winter?
- 2. Look at the graph on page 209. Which bird has fewer baby birds each spring than the other birds?
3. Why do you think people enjoy feeding hummingbirds?
- 4. Look at the graph on page 211. Which bird is almost as small as a hummingbird?
5. What did you learn about hummingbirds that surprised you the most?

Talking About What You've Read

Name three things that you think most people don't know about hummingbirds.

Writing About What You've Read

Imagine you're putting together a book about birds. List three things about hummingbirds that you would put on the "Hummingbird" page.

- Study Skills: Graphs

To be read by the teacher

from Getting Ready
by Aileen Fisher

Now bluebirds look at timetables
and swallows check their maps
and warblers pack their suitcases
and buckle all the straps.

Now frogs and turtles hide themselves
down under mud and ooze . . .
and WE go dig our earmuffs out
and skis and overshoes.

LOOKING BACK

Thinking About the Section

You have read about many different kinds of birds. You read about nests that birds build, about birds that fly to warm places, and about the hummingbird that flies many ways.

Think about how birds look and what they do. On your own paper, list the birds on the left. Then write something you know about each bird. Use your book if you need help.

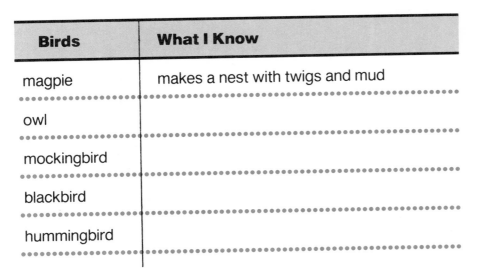

Birds	What I Know
magpie	makes a nest with twigs and mud
owl	
mockingbird	
blackbird	
hummingbird	

Writing About the Section

Pick the bird you liked the best and write a few sentences about it.

6

Something Special

Think of all the people and things that are special to you. Something special to you might be something you collect or a special friend. What is special about you?

Look at the pictures on pages 220–257 to find out what you will read about. Look for things or people that you think are special.

Learning About Maps and Globes

When you visit a place you have never been before, you might need some help to find your way around. You may need to use a map to help you find your way.

A **map** is a special drawing of real places and things. A map tells you everything you need to know so you can find out where something is. The pictures on the map stand for real things. Look at the map. A map has a key. The **key** tells what the pictures on the map stand for. A **globe** is a map that is round, like the earth. Look at the map on the next page to answer the questions.

Use the map to answer the questions.

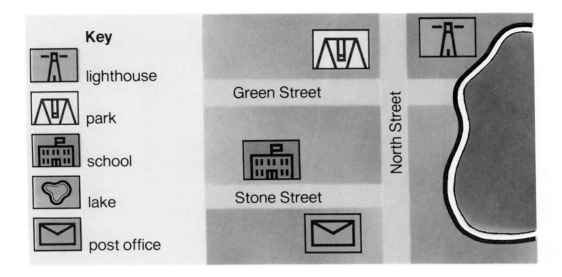

1. What picture tells you where the park is?

If you said the swing, you were right. The key tells you that the picture of the swing stands for the park.

2. What building is next to the lake?

If you said the lighthouse, you were right. The key tells you what the pictures stand for. The lighthouse is next to the lake.

3. What picture stands for the post office?
4. What is across from the post office?

Practicing with Maps

Look at the map to find out where things are.

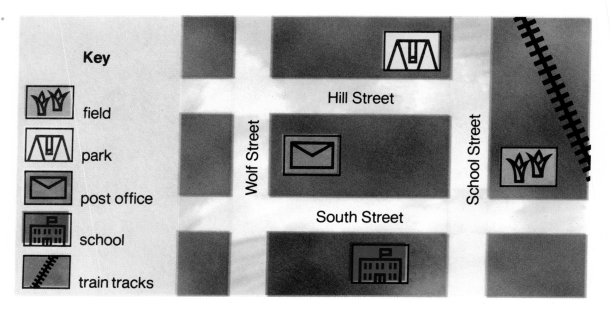

1. What is in the middle of the map?
2. What passes through the field?

Tips for Reading Maps on Your Own

- Remember that the pictures on a map stand for real things and places.
- Look at the map key to find out what the pictures stand for.

Too Many Books!

by Caroline Feller Bauer

Maralou really liked books. As a baby, she liked books.

When Maralou learned to read, she read all of the time. She read at the breakfast table. She read on the bus to school. She read when she took a bath. She would try to read as she jumped rope.

Every Wednesday, Maralou went to the library to borrow books. The following Wednesday, Maralou took the books back and borrowed more.

One day during Book Week, Aunt Molly gave Maralou a book as a gift. Great! Now that she owned her own book, she could read it over and over again.

Maralou wanted more books. She asked for books every time someone wanted to give her a gift.

Maralou got books for many special days. She never knew when she would be surprised with another book.

Maralou worked hard so she could buy books. She cat sat. She made cold drinks to sell. She sold old clothes that didn't fit her. She wanted to sell her little brother, but that didn't work.

After some time, Maralou had bought many, many books. Mom and Dad had to build a place for the books but there still wasn't enough room.

There were books in the tub, on every table, all over her room, and in the kitchen too.

Maralou had bought too many books! Mom could not get out the front door. Dad could not get in the back door. But Maralou still really liked books and wanted more to read. How could she make room?

Then Maralou had a thought. Maybe other people would like books too! So she planned to give some books away. She gave a book to a little boy on his way to school. She gave a book to the mail carrier. She left books at the museum and at school on the swings.

Soon the whole town was reading all the time. People bought books, borrowed books, and traded books. The town was stuffed with books. The head of the town called the people who worked in the library of the next town. He wanted to see if they would like to have some books.

They did, and it wasn't long before *all* the towns close by were borrowing and trading and reading and sharing books.

But Maralou didn't see this. She sat in front of the library reading a book.

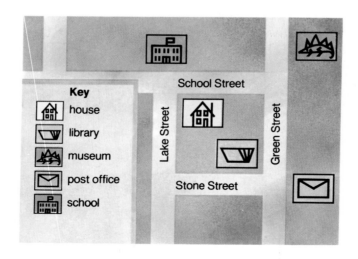

The Library

by Sallie Runck

This is the **library.** It is a place near
you where you can borrow books. To be able
to use your town's library, you must show
that you live in that town and you must
follow the library's rules.

The library has all kinds of books. There
are books about people, places, and things
at the library. There are books that tell
how to make gifts and books that can be
read just for fun. The library has books
with large letters for people who can't
see well.

The library will lend more than just books to people. It may lend tape recorders and tapes or passes to a **museum.** A family may use these passes to visit a museum for a day. Your library may have other things it lends to people.

This library has many different rooms. One room has big tables. People come here to work and read. Another room is used by the people of the town to hold meetings. Another room is used to read to children. Every Wednesday morning children can hear a new story read.

This is the children's room. It looks like a classroom, but it has more books than a classroom. On the walls are letters from writers telling children why they like to write books. There are a few letters from the people who draw pictures for books too.

Ann and Dan were going to borrow a few books. They knew they should look for books in the children's room. Ann found a book on puppets to borrow. Dan found a book of cartoons. Dan thinks this will be the best book of cartoons he has found yet. After two weeks, the children will take the books back and borrow a few more.

Books borrowed this week

Ann	📖 📖 📖 📖
Bill	📖 📖
Rose	📖
Dan	📖 📖 📖

📖 = 1 Book

The library is the best place to find out about things. This girl likes to collect rocks. She wants to find out more about the rocks she collects. She wasn't surprised to find a book on rocks at the library. She knew the library was the best place to look.

The library is really a special place. Learn what the rules are at the library near you. Then you can find all of the things inside the library that are there for you to borrow.

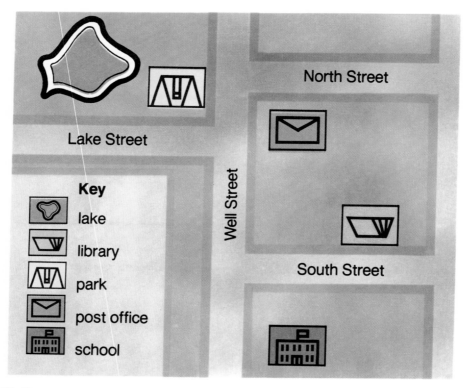

North Street

Lake Street

Well Street

South Street

Key

lake

library

park

post office

school

Checking Comprehension and Skills

Thinking About What You've Read

1. In "Too Many Books," why does Maralou ask for more books?
2. Why do you think Maralou likes to read so much?
• 3. On the map on page 228, what building is the closest to the post office?
4. What are some things you may find in the library?
• 5. On the map on page 232, what picture stands for the library?
6. What kinds of books do you like to read?

Talking About What You've Read

Maralou likes to collect books. Talk about different things people collect. Then tell why people might collect them.

Writing About What You've Read

Write three sentences about something you would like to collect. Tell why you think it would be fun to collect.

• Study Skill: Maps and globes

Reading

by Marchette Chute

A story is a special thing.
   The ones that I have read,
They do not stay inside the books.
   They stay inside my head.

Meet the Poet

  Marchette Chute writes poems for
children. Before she writes a poem, she
remembers things she liked as a little girl.

  Marchette Chute has always enjoyed books.
She remembers her first trip to a library.
She was surprised at everything there was to
learn from books. Her poem "Reading" tells
you how much she likes to remember the
things she has read.

Little Otter's Coasting Party

by Ann Tompert

Little Otter flopped on his stomach and went sliding down the hill of snow. Then Mother Otter went sliding down the hill and stopped right next to him.

"Let's do it again," said Little Otter.

"Let's," said his mother.

Mother Otter and Little Otter went sliding down the hill until it was as smooth as glass.

"It would be fun to have a coasting party," said Little Otter.

"Who would come?" asked Mother Otter.

"I will ask all my friends," said Little Otter.

"Good," said Mother Otter. "You ask your friends and I will make popcorn."

Mother Otter fixed Little Otter's hat and gave him a kiss. Then he rushed off.

When Little Otter came to Woodchuck's house, he tapped at the door. There was no answer. Just as Little Otter turned to leave, Skunk opened the door.

"What do you want?" Skunk asked.

"Is Woodchuck home?" asked Little Otter.

"Yes," said Skunk, "but he is sleeping. He plans to sleep until spring." Then Skunk closed the door in Little Otter's face.

"Skunk can be a crab," said Raccoon who was sitting in a tree close by.

"No one wants to come to my coasting party," said Little Otter.

"A coasting party!" shouted Raccoon. "That sounds like fun."

"Would you come?" asked Little Otter.

"Yes," said Raccoon.

Just then clouds moved into the sky. It grew darker and darker.

"It is going to snow," said Raccoon. "I do not like snow. I am going home until it is over." Raccoon rushed off.

A few snowflakes floated down. "I must go home too," Little Otter said.

The snow fell faster and faster. Soon it was hard for Little Otter to see where he was going. Snow fell all around him.

As Little Otter came near his home, the snow stopped falling. He was surprised at what he saw. All of his cousins and aunts were coasting on the hill.

"We have come to your party," one of his aunts called.

"Great!" shouted Little Otter.

Little Otter's mother and aunts coasted down the slide on their stomachs many times. Little Otter's cousins coasted down the slide on their stomachs many times too. But Little Otter was so happy that he coasted down the slide more times than any of his cousins or his aunts.

Best Friends

by Nancy Ross Ryan

On Monday afternoon Angela's teacher said, "Class, we are going to put on a play. I wrote the parts down on paper and put them in this hat. One at a time, you may pick your part from the hat."

When it was Angela's turn, she put her hand into the hat and pulled out the paper with the words <u>Snow Queen</u> on it. Angela had really wanted that part all along.

That night Angela didn't want to save her news. "Guess what happened today," she said to her grandma. "I am going to be the Snow Queen in the class play."

Angela wanted everyone to be really proud of her, so she practiced every afternoon. One afternoon as she practiced, her cousin Donna came over. Donna was Angela's cousin and her best friend too. She was always there when Angela needed help. Today Donna helped her fix her costume so it would look just right.

Donna's class was going to work behind the stage with the lights and music.

The big night came at last. "I guess I know my part," Angela said. "I have been practicing since Monday."

"If you have practiced since Monday, you will not have a problem doing your best. We are all proud of your hard work," Angela's mother said. "Your dad will be home from downtown soon. It will be time to go. Come along and help Grandma and me fix the popcorn for the party after the play."

Angela and Donna walked along on their way to school with the bag of popcorn. Then their problems began. Angela tripped over a branch and the popcorn fell all over.

"Oh, no!" said Angela. "Now we have a problem. Since we can't eat the popcorn, we don't have anything to take to the party. It's too late to get anything now."

"It doesn't matter," said Donna. "Let's clean up this mess. Here, put the popcorn back in the bag."

When the girls got to school, Angela went to her teacher and told her about the problem. The teacher said it didn't matter. The popcorn wasn't a problem.

Just then Donna had a thought. "We don't have anything to eat, but I can still put this popcorn to good use," Donna said.

The play started. Angela walked on the stage in her costume. Then zap! Soft, white snowflakes started falling on the stage.

Angela's family was proud of her as she remembered all her lines. But they could not guess where the snowflakes had come from.

No one knew that Donna was behind the stage. She was busy making snow by throwing the old popcorn over Angela, the Snow Queen.

It didn't matter that there wasn't any popcorn to eat at the party, because everyone said the snow was great. Angela's best friend had helped her again. Donna had helped make the whole night very special.

Checking Comprehension and Skills

Thinking About What You've Read

1. What does Little Otter want to have? Does he get it?
2. Why do you think Little Otter is so happy to see his aunts and cousins?
- 3. Is "Little Otter's Coasting Party" a real story or a make-believe story? What helps you to know?
4. What does Donna do to help Angela?
- 5. Is "Best Friends" a real story or a make-believe story? What helps you to know?
6. Why do you think having a friend is special?

Talking About What You've Read

Angela and Little Otter know special people. Tell about some of the special people you know at school. Then tell why they are special.

Writing About What You've Read

Write three sentences about someone at school who is special to you. Tell why he or she is special.

- Comprehension: Realism and fantasy

The Ugly Duckling

adapted by Nancy Ross Ryan from
a tale by Hans Christian Andersen

Two fine ducks lived near the pond on a
farm. Each spring they were very busy with
their nest. The mother duck sat on her eggs
to keep them warm. The father duck brought
her food to eat.

"When will the eggs be ready to open?" the
father duck wondered. "How many ducklings
will there be?"

One day the farmer found an egg by the
pond. "Look what I found," he said. "I guess
this egg rolled out of the mother duck's
nest. I'll just put it back when she
takes her walk. She will never know it
was missing."

Then the farmer hid the egg in the nest.

That night the mother duck felt the eggs stir. "It won't be long now," she said. "I think we will be seeing ducklings soon."

By morning the eggs began to open. One yellow duckling pushed its way out into the sun. Another duckling climbed out of its egg. Soon there were five little ducklings.

"Oh, what pretty ducklings," the mother duck said.

"They are as fine as can be," the proud father said.

"But what is this?" the mother duck asked. "This big egg has not opened yet."

The mother duck sat down upon the nest again. Soon other ducks came to visit. The old goose came to watch the egg open too.

"You never can tell," the old goose said to the mother duck. "Maybe someone played a trick on you and put a different egg in your nest!"

"Maybe it's an owl's egg," said one duck.

"Maybe it's one of the goose's eggs," said another duck.

"Maybe it's a snake's egg," said yet another duck.

At last the big egg began to open and the last duckling rolled out. The last duckling didn't look anything like the other ducklings. He wasn't little and yellow but big and gray. This duckling was not small and pretty. He was large and funny-looking.

"Oh, my!" the mother duck said. "You are such an ugly duckling. Maybe you are not a duckling after all, and you are too ugly to be a goose. Let's go down to the pond to see if you can swim. If you are a duck, you will swim. If you are an owl or a chicken, you won't be able to swim."

The mother duck started out for the pond. She was the first in line, waddling along on her big, flat feet. The little yellow ducklings followed along on their little, flat feet. The ugly duckling was at the end.

The mother duck was the first one in the pond. Then splash! The ugly duckling jumped in as the other ducklings just watched.

"Won't you join us in the pond?" the mother duck asked the other ducklings. "Come right in, the water is fine."

The little yellow ducklings jumped in. They, too, could swim, but the ugly duckling was the best swimmer. Now the mother duck knew he belonged to her.

"Come along, children," the mother duck said to all the ducklings. "It is time to meet the other animals. Now watch your father and walk as he does, with your feet turned out. Remember, the old goose is queen of the farm. When you meet her, bend your neck. Bend your neck and bow."

The farm animals looked at the new ducklings. "What an ugly duckling that one is," a goose said. "Is it really a duckling?"

"It is a duckling," the mother duck said. "He is very clever. Out of all my ducklings, he is the best swimmer and I think he is cute."

As the days went by, the ugly duckling grew sad. Nobody would play with him. Everyone made fun of him. All the animals called him the ugly duckling. When the farmer fed the animals, the ugly duckling was always the last to eat.

"I am so ugly, I don't have any friends," the ugly duckling said. "I am going to fly away. It won't matter if I leave, since I am always so alone."

The ugly duckling left the farm and didn't say good-by. He lived alone as the days grew colder. He sometimes felt afraid, sometimes hungry, but he always felt alone.

One day the ugly duckling came upon a flock of beautiful birds. The great birds had long necks, and feathers as white as snow. Their beaks were as black as night.

The duckling wanted to talk to the birds, but they spread their wings to fly. As they flew away, they gave out a loud cry. The cry made the ugly duckling want to join them. When the beautiful birds had left, the ugly duckling felt more alone than before.

Winter came at last. Since it was so cold, the ugly duckling could no longer swim in the lake. The duckling walked until he found a little house where an old man, his wife, a cat, and an old chicken lived. They took the ugly duckling in.

The ugly duckling was safe and warm, but he missed the water. He told the cat about the deep, blue lake and the beautiful birds.

"Don't tell me anything about water," the cat sniffed. "I never get wet."

"Don't tell me anything about water either," the chicken said. "I don't swim."

When spring came, the duckling said good-by to the man and his wife. The ugly duckling knew he had to go back to the lake.

The duckling spread his wings and flew away. The sun was bright, the air was warm.

"If only I had a friend," the ugly duckling thought.

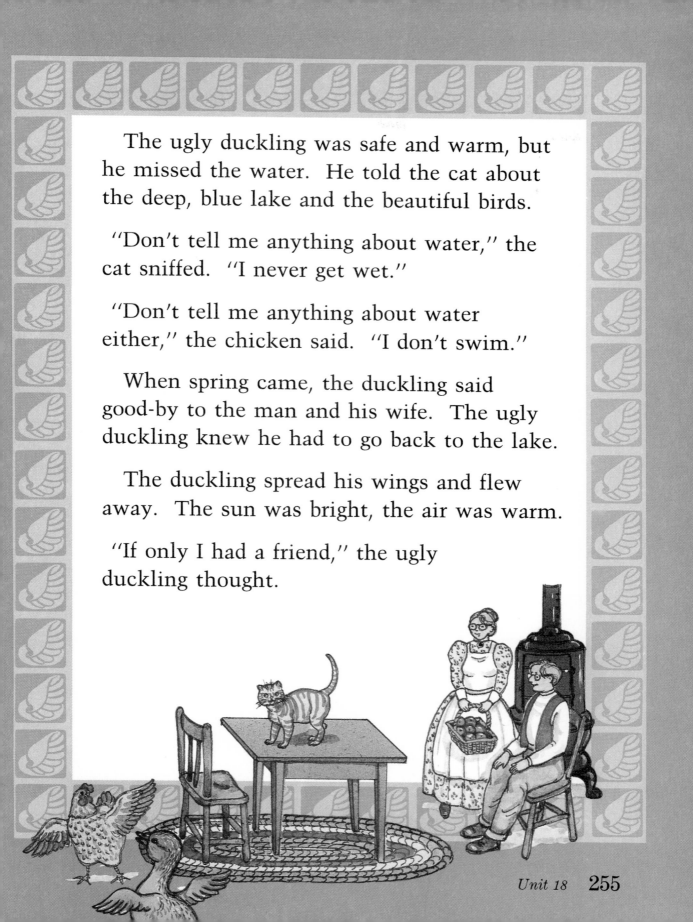

At the lake the duckling saw the beautiful birds again. The duckling asked one of them, "What kind of bird are you?"

"Why, I am a swan just like you," the white bird said. "Won't you come along with us since you are alone? You are so beautiful you could be the prince of all the swans."

The ugly duckling knew the swan was joking. The duckling bowed his head. Then the duckling saw himself in the water.

What a surprise! The duckling was a beautiful swan. How happy he was! He had never been an ugly duckling. All along he had been a baby swan. So off he went to join the other swans.

Meet the Author

Hans Christian Andersen lived a long time ago, but people still enjoy reading every story he wrote. Most of Mr. Andersen's books are for children, but moms and dads like to read them too.

Mr. Andersen wrote "The Ugly Duckling" because he felt different from other children when he was a boy. He thought he was like an ugly duckling. When Mr. Andersen grew up, he wrote beautiful books.

Mr. Andersen's story, "The Ugly Duckling," has been told by many different people. Each time the story is told, it is a little different than before. People enjoy telling this story again and again.

You might enjoy reading another story by Hans Christian Andersen, such as "The Snow Queen" or "The Red Shoes."

LOOKING BACK

Thinking About the Section

You have read about how the things Maralou likes to collect make her special. You read about how the library is a special place.

Think about the other special people and things you read about in this section. Finish the sentences to tell what was special in each story.

1. Little Otter has a special day when
2. Donna is Angela's special friend because
3. The special thing that the ugly duckling learns is

Writing About the Section

One way you can share something special is by writing a letter to a special friend. Tell your friend what you think is special in one story.

Books to Read

Clams Can't Sing
by James Stevenson

All the animals down at the sea are making music. Two small animals are told to just listen. Read to find out what the two small animals do.

Benedict Finds a Home
by Chris L. Demarest

Benedict is a bird who wants to be alone. He leaves his busy nest to find a new nest all his own. Read to find out where Benedict's new home is.

It's Me, Claudia!
by Alyse Newman

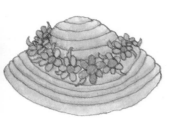

Claudia thinks her ears are <u>too</u> big! She tries to hide them in many ways. Find out how a big, floppy hat helps Claudia learn what makes her special to her friends.

To be read by the teacher

On the next few pages are some of the strategies you've learned to figure out the meaning and pronunciation of words.

Phonics: Consonant Sounds and Letters

Strategy 1: I can use what I know about **consonant sounds and letters** at the beginning, middle, and end of a word.

Say these words:

build	**c**arrot	twi**g**
pink	gi**gg**le	o**x**
meat	ra**bb**it	feet

Vocabulary and Skill Application

Write the sentences. Use the words from the box to complete the sentences.

1. Dave thinks his new pet ____ is cute.
2. He is small and has ____ ears.
3. He hops around on two big ____.
4. He likes Dave to give him a ____ to eat.
5. Dave wants to ____ a home for his pet.
6. Dave's new pet makes him ____ and smile.

To be read by the teacher

Phonics: Blends

Strategy 2: I can use what I know about two- or three-letter **blends** at the beginning or end of a word.

Say these words. Listen to the sounds of the two or three letters blended together at the beginning or end of each word.

cross	**dr**ess	be**st**	li**st**
throw	**sw**amp	gi**ft**	so**ft**
slide	**fr**ont	ju**st**	ki**nd**
clothes	**spl**ash	le**nd**	sou**nd**

Vocabulary and Skill Application

Write the sentences. Use the words from the box to complete the sentences.

1. Dad and I gave Mom a birthday ＿＿＿.
2. It was a pretty red ＿＿＿ and shoes.
3. There was a bow on the ＿＿＿ of the dress.
4. We saw the clothes on Mom's birthday ＿＿＿.
5. We hoped they would be ＿＿＿ what she liked.
6. Mom said her new ＿＿＿ were special.
7. She thought we were very ＿＿＿.

See also Skill Lesson: 3-Letter Blends on pages 163–164.

Phonics: Digraphs

Strategy 3: I can use what I know about **digraphs** that stand for one sound at the beginning or end of a word.

Say these words. Listen to the sound of the two letters that stand for one sound at the beginning or end of each word.

shy	**qu**ills	nor**th**	bu**sh**
chew	**th**ought	ear**th**	mu**ch**
thing	**sh**irt	bran**ch**	tou**ch**
shout	**wh**ich	thru**sh**	tee**th**

Vocabulary and Skill Application

Write the sentences. Use the words from the box to complete the sentences.

1. Sam ___ he saw a porcupine.
2. It was near a ___ in the woods.
3. Sam saw it ___ on a ___.
4. He started to ___ to tell his friend Rob.
5. Rob was ___ too busy looking up in a tree.
6. "What is that ___ up there?" asked Sam.
7. Rob said, "The bird is called a ___."
8. They did not know ___ one to watch.

Phonics: Short Vowel Sounds

Strategy 4: I can use what I know about **short vowel sounds** in a one-syllable word.

Say these words. Listen to the vowel sound in each word. What kind of letters are before and after the vowel in each word?

Short *a*	Short *e*	Short *i*	Short *o*	Short *u*
nap	leg	hid	dot	mud
flat	wet	kiss	flop	hung
plant	fed	flip	rock	bumpy
splash	nest	spin	sock	lunch

Vocabulary and Skill Application

Write the sentences. Use the words from the box to complete the sentences.

1. Beth got ____ in the rain.
2. Her shoes had ____ all over them.
3. There was a small ____ of mud on her face.
4. Her friends wanted to ____ in the water.
5. Beth wanted to go home and ____ into bed.
6. When she got home her mom gave her a ____.
7. Beth ____ up her wet clothes right away.
8. Then, Beth's mom ____ her some hot soup.
9. At last, Beth went to bed and took a ____.

Phonics: Long Vowel Sounds
Strategy 5: I can use what I know about **long vowel sounds** in a one-syllable word.

Say these words. Listen to the vowel sounds. Which words have two vowels together that stand for a long vowel sound? Which words have a vowel and a consonant followed by the letter *e*?

Long *a*	Long *e*	Long *i*	Long *o*	Long *u*
safe	feet	pine	wrote	tune
stay	sea	slide	close	rule
pail	deep	wife	soap	tube

Vocabulary and Skill Application

Write the sentences. Use the words from the box to complete the sentences.

1. Rick likes to ____ at his friend's house.
2. His friend Al lives near the ____.
3. Rick and Al are very ____ friends.
4. When Rick visits he brings his water ____.
5. Al's mom has a ____ about the water.
6. They can't swim and play in the ____ water.
7. Rick and Al play only where it is ____.
8. They like to run and ____ in the water.

Phonics: r-controlled Vowels

Strategy 6: I can use what I know about **r-controlled vowels.**

Say these words. Listen to the vowel sounds.
What letter comes after the vowel in each
word?

far	her	girl	or	turn
dark	germ	stir	sport	curve
star	perch	shirt	north	purple
large	were	circle	work	burner

Vocabulary and Skill Application

Write the sentences. Use the words from
the box to complete the sentences.

1. Val watched a show on the ___ TV.
2. A man with a red ___ was on the show.
3. He always talked about birds ___ trees.
4. Today they ___ going to talk about birds.
5. There was a bird on a ___ next to him.
6. The bird had green and ___ feathers.
7. The man told it to ___ around and dance.
8. The bird had so much ___ to do on TV.

See also Skill Lesson: r-controlled Vowels on pages 81–83.

Phonics: Vowel Sounds

Strategy 7: I can use what I know about **vowel sounds.**

Say these words. Listen to the vowel sounds. What letters stand for the vowel sounds in each word?		

<table>
<tr><td>loud</td><td>bow</td><td>boy</td></tr>
<tr><td>found</td><td>owl</td><td>noise</td></tr>
<tr><td>proud</td><td>low</td><td>point</td></tr>
<tr><td>brought</td><td>frown</td><td>enjoy</td></tr>
</table>

Vocabulary and Skill Application

Write the sentences. Use the words from the box to complete the sentences.

1. Dad ____ a duck near the lake.
2. He ____ the duck over to me.
3. The duck made a funny ____ .
4. It was a ____ noise.
5. Dad started to ____ .
6. I saw Dad ____ to the duck's leg.
7. Once, Dad helped an ____ with a bad wing.
8. He told me I was a good ____ .
9. I am very ____ of my dad.

Structure: Endings

Strategy 8: I can use what I know about **endings** added to a root word with and without spelling changes.

A. Add endings *-s*, *-es*, *-ed*, *-ing* without changing the root word:

*open   open*s   *open*ed   *open*ing

B. Drop the *e* and add endings *-ed* or *-ing*:

shine   shine + **ing** = *shin***ing**

C. Double the last consonant and add endings *-ed* or *-ing*:

tap + p + **ed** = *tap***ed**   *tap***ing**

Vocabulary and Skill Application

Write the words. Add the endings. Complete the sentences with the words you make.

Add *-s*	Add *-es*	Add *-ed*	Add *-ing*
shouts	watch**es**	stopp**ed**	rid**ing**
eye	dress	comb	climb
plan	hatch	trip	taste

1. Ana thought about ＿＿ out of bed.
2. She rolled over and opened her ＿＿.
3. She got out of bed and ＿＿ her hair.
4. Ana put on one of her ＿＿ and left.

America

arm

Glossary

A a

afraid   not feeling safe: *Are you afraid of snakes?*
America   a country. See the picture.
arm   the part of you next to your hand. See the picture. **arms**
audience   people together in one place to hear or see something: *The audience liked the singer.* **audiences**
aunt   your father or mother's sister: *My mother's sister, Ruth, is my aunt.* **aunts**

B b

beak

backward   with the back first: *Walk backward.*
beak   the mouth of a bird. See the picture. **beaks**
blind   not able to see: *The man with the seeing eye dog is blind.*
borrow   get something from someone to use just for a little time: *He wants to borrow my book.* **borrows borrowed borrowing**
busy   working: *He is a busy man.*

C c

cello   something someone plays to make pretty sounds. See the picture. **cellos**

clever   bright; a good thinker: *She is a clever girl.*

cliff   a high hill of rock. See the picture. **cliffs**

climb   go up something too hard to walk up: *I climbed a tree.* **climbs climbed climbing**

costume   clothes; what someone puts on when they are in a play: *In our play I had on a king's costume.* **costumes**

cousin   your aunt's children: *My cousin and I are best friends.* **cousins**

cello

cliff

D d

dark   without light: *It is dark at night.*

deep   going a long way down from the top: *That hole is deep.*

duckling   a baby duck. See the picture. **ducklings**

dye   something that water is added to that can be used to color clothes, hair, and other things. **dyes**

duckling

269

E e

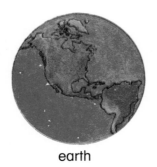

earth

each   every one: *Each boy in the class has his lunch with him.*

earth   the ground on which we live, a great ball that moves around the sun. See the picture.

enjoy   be happy or have fun with: *We enjoy playing games.* **enjoys enjoyed enjoying**

F f

few   not many: *There are a few pieces of fruit left.*

finish   bring to an end; get to the end of: *Finish your work before you go out to play.* **finishes finished finishing**

flow   run like water: *The river flows into the lake.* **flows flowed flowing**

funny   something that makes you laugh: *The man's funny jokes made us laugh.*

G g

gray

giggle   a kind of laugh: *We could hear a loud giggle from the back of the room.* **giggles**

gray   a color made by putting black and white together. See the picture. **grays**

H h

high   tall: *The bird is flying high over the tree tops.*

hold   take or pick up and keep: *Hold this book for me.* **holds holding**

hole   an open place: *There is a big hole in this sock.* **holes**

hummingbird   a tiny, brightly colored bird. See the picture. **hummingbirds**

hungry   feeling a need for food: *The girls are hungry.*

hummingbird

I i

insect   a small animal with six legs and, many times, with four wings: *Flies and bees are insects.* **insects**

inside   the part not on the outside: *It was warm inside the house.* **insides**

J j

join   bring things together: *We joined hands in a circle.* **joins joined joining**

joke   something funny said or done to make people laugh: *Looking for the hat that was on my head was a good joke on me.* **jokes**

K k

kitchen   a room where food is cooked. See the picture. **kitchens**

kitchen

L l

lend let someone use something you own: *I will lend you my pencil.* **lends lending**

less not much: *We have less shade since the tree was cut down.*

loom something used to weave with. See the picture. **looms**

loud not soft; making a great sound: *When the door shut it made a loud noise.*

low not high or tall: *This is a low table.*

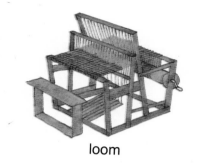

loom

M m

middle not on the left or right: *The middle house is ours.*

mockingbird a bird that sounds like other birds. It is the state bird of many states. See the picture. **mockingbirds**

Monday the second day of the week: *We are going to the city on Monday.* **Mondays**

morning the first part of the day: *He gets up at six o'clock every morning.* **mornings**

museum the building or rooms in which you can see things that have been collected: *Our class saw paintings at the museum.* **museums**

mockingbird

N n

nap sleep for a little time: *The baby takes a nap after lunch.* **naps napped napping**

near close to; not far from: *We live near a city.*

nobody no one: *When people were told about the bear, nobody wanted to go for a walk in the woods.*

nose the part of your face that lets you smell: *My dog's nose is always cold.* **noses**

octopus

O o

octopus a sea animal with eight arms. See the picture. **octopuses**

opossum a small animal that puts its baby on its back. See the picture. **opossums**

our belonging to us: *We painted our house.*

owl a bird with big eyes that looks for food at night. See the picture. **owls**

ox an animal that is fitted and trained for farm work. See the picture. **oxen**

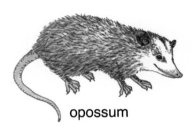

opossum

owl

P p

piece one part, one thing: *I can't find one piece of my game.* **pieces**

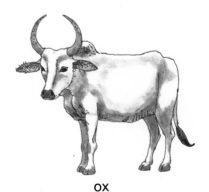

ox

pine

quill

raccoon

shirt

pine a tree with leaves that are always green and shaped like needles. See the picture. **pines**

popcorn a kind of food that opens up when it gets hot: *Popcorn is good to eat.*

proud thinking well of something: *He is proud of his children.*

Q q

quill a large, hard feather. See the picture. **quills**

R r

raccoon a small animal that moves around at night. See the picture. **raccoons**

roof the top of a building: *The roof on my house is red.* **roofs**

round shaped like a ball or a circle: *The earth is round.*

S s

second next after the first: *She finished second in the race.*

shirt a piece of clothing. See the picture. **shirts**

sister a girl with the same mother and father as another: *My sister and I have brown hair and green eyes.* **sisters**

small not large: *A mouse is a small animal.*

sound what you hear: *I can hear the sound of music.* **sounds**

sport a kind of game: *Bowling is a sport.* **sports**

stage the place where a show is put on. See the picture. **stages**

swamp wet, soft ground. See the picture. **swamps**

swan a large bird with a long, curving neck. **swans**

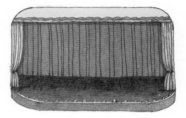

stage

T t

talk use words: *The baby is learning to talk.* **talks talked talking**

tall high: *New York has many tall buildings.*

tape a piece of something used to tie things together: *I fixed the pages with tape.* **tapes**

tiny very small: *The kittens are tiny.*

swamp

U u

until up to the time of: *He waited until dark to go to bed.*

275

V v

visit   go to see; come to see: *Are you going to visit your aunt?* **visits   visited   visiting**

voice   sounds made through the throat and mouth: *His voice is very deep.* **voices**

W w

Wednesday   the day of the week after Tuesday: *I go to the library every Wednesday.* **Wednesdays**

wet   not dry: *After it rains, the ground is wet.*

wide   big from side to side: *We crossed a wide river.*

woodpecker   a bird with a hard, pointed beak for making holes in trees to get insects. See the picture. **woodpeckers**

wool   the soft hair on sheep: *A weaver spins wool into yarn.*

woodpecker

Y y

year   the time the earth takes to go around the sun once: *It will take me a year to finish that building.* **years**

Z z

zigzag   short turns from one side to the other: *We ran in a zigzag through the field.*

Word List

Unit 1
night 17
dark 17
list 21
morning 21
remember 21
wrote 21
paper 21
wake 22
cross 22
dress 22
nap 22
clothes 23
soon 24
took 24
hello 24
long 25
high 25
shout 25
catch 26
swamp 26

Unit 2
nighttime 31
chew 31
berries 31
baby 32
opossum 32
shine 32
raccoon 32
beaver 33
through 33
teeth 33
branch 33
porcupine 34
pine 34
quill 34
waddle 34

bush 34
hear 36
noise 36
afraid 36
fell 37
rabbit 37
hole 38

Unit 3
year 42
earth 42
visit 42
answer 43
push 43
enough 43
room 43
build 44
large 44
plant 44
wife 44
began 45
done 45
until 46
safe 46
flow 47
wet 47
deep 47
head 48
roof 48

Unit 4
touch 53
feel 53
grandpa 57
blind 57
exercise 58
close 58

voice 58
kitchen 58
plate 59
food 59
o'clock 59
cello 60
tune 60
finger 60
slide 60
listen 60
clay 62
face 63
lunch 64
dot 64
word 64
funny 64
kiss 65

Unit 5
goat 69
window 69
rock 69
weave 70
wool 70
piece 70
stay 70
soap 71
pail 71
hung 71
comb 72
each 72
spin 72
pull 72
dye 73
turn 75
pink 75
our 76

pole 76
loom 76

Unit 6
sport 83
shirt 83
curve 83
perch 83
or 83
star 83
every 84
kind 84
milk 84
Saturday 86
bowl 86
practice 87
plan 87
puppet 88
costume 88
talk 88
add 89
lip 89
hair 89
stage 90

Unit 7
great 95
country 99
bicycle 99
chase 99
second 99
week 99
air 100
launch 100
shortcut 100
before 101

ready   101
front   101
woman   101
thought   102
helper   102
roll   102
burner   103
tall   103
rope   103
nobody   104
bull   106
caught   107

Unit 8
surprise   110
been   110
canary   110
cage   110
tie   111
taller   111
watchdog   112
middle   112
never   113
hungry   113
hardest   113
manners   113
felt   114
belong   115
tea   115
biscuit   115
table   115
himself   115
singer   116
dead   116
ate   117
same   119
tail   120

Unit 9
stone   125
soup   125

far   125
soldier   125
hid   126
bit   126
potato   127
carrot   127
meat   127
everyone   129
stir   130

Unit 10
joke   137
cartoon   137
pencil   141
able   141
circle   141
ear   142
inside   142
tiny   142
nose   142
page   143
Tuesday   143
birthday   143
once   144
nice   144
giant   144
busy   146
audience   146
TV   146
during   147
whole   148
age   148
wide   148

Unit 11
socks   152
ox   152
bumpy   152
grumpy   152

less   153
rid   153
shoes   153
feet   153
flip   154
flop   154
leg   154
clever   154
hold   155
giggle   155
golden   156
goose   156
storyteller   157
father   157
gray   157
sister   160
stuck   160
king   161

Unit 12
sailor   165
wonder   165
storm   165
might   165
sea   166
small   166
wave   166
splash   166
scream   167
should   167
strong   168
shark   168
zigzag   169
throw   169
across   169
sail   170
octopus   170
arm   170
cliff   172
everything   174

Unit 13
nest   179
enjoy   179
magpie   183
teach   183
round   183
thrush   183
turtledove   184
brought   184
twig   184
blackbird   184
wise   185
owl   185
starling   185
soft   185
watch   186
finish   186
except   186
pillow   187
behind   188
point   190

Unit 14
mockingbird   193
care   193
bright   194
warm   194
wing   194
low   195
among   196
grass   196
sound   196
grew   197
loud   197
woodpecker   198
climb   198
insect   198
beak   198
near   198
farther   198

frown 199
angry 200
alone 200

Unit 15
winter 206
north 206
few 206
south 206
hummingbird 207
maybe 207
either 207
dry 207
flock 208
hurry 209
hatch 209
trip 209
flies 210
ago 210
shy 210
throat 210
taste 211
backward 213

Unit 16
collect 219
really 223
Wednesday 224
library 224
borrow 224
gift 224
knew 225
another 225
didn't 225
bought 226
wasn't 226
museum 227
letter 229
lend 230
tape 230

classroom 231
wall 231
found 231
best 231

Unit 17
coast 235
party 235
stomach 235
popcorn 236
fix 236
snowflake 238
cousin 239
aunt 239
Monday 240
afternoon 240
along 240
save 241
guess 241
grandma 241
proud 241
since 242
problem 242
downtown 242
anything 243
matter 243

Unit 18
ugly 247
duckling 247
won't 248
pretty 248
flat 251
end 251
join 251
bend 252
neck 252
bow 252
good-by 253
beautiful 254
swan 256

Page 110: *A Pet for Duck and Bear* by Judy Delton. Text copyright © 1982 by Judy Delton. Illustrations copyright © 1982 by Lynn Munsinger. Adapted by permission of Albert Whitman & Company.

Page 123: "Changing" from *Yellow Butter Purple Jelly Red Jam Black Bread* by Mary Ann Hoberman. Copyright © 1981 by Mary Ann Hoberman. Reprinted by permission of Viking Penguin Inc.

Page 152: *"There Are Rocks in My Socks!" Said the Ox to the Fox* by Patricia Thomas. Text Copyright © 1979 by Patricia Thomas. Abridged and adapted by permission of Lothrop, Lee & Shepard Books (A Division of William Morrow). Illustrations on pp. 6, 7, 10, 11, 34, and 35 by Mordicai Gerstein. Copyright © 1979 by Mordicai Gerstein. By permission of Lothrop, Lee & Shepard Books (A Division of William Morrow).

Page 176: "Fish Song" from *Nibble, Nibble: Poems for Children* by Margaret Wise Brown (A Young-Scott Book). Text copyright © 1959 by William R. Scott. Reprinted by permission of Harper & Row, Publishers, Inc.

Page 187: "Goose Feathers" adapted by permission of Alfred A. Knopf, Inc. from *The Topsy-Turvy Family*, by Emma L. Brock. Copyright 1943 and renewed 1971 by Emma L. Brock.

Page 216: From "Getting Ready" in *Runny Days Sunny Days* by Aileen Fisher. Copyright © 1933, 1938, 1946, 1958 by Aileen Fisher. Reprinted by permission of the author.

Page 223: From *Too Many Books!* by Caroline Feller Bauer, illustrated by Diane Paterson. Text copyright © 1984 by Caroline Feller Bauer. Illustrations copyright © 1984 by Diane Paterson. Adapted by permission of Viking Penguin, Inc.

Page 234: "Reading" from *Rhymes About Us* by Marchette Chute. Copyright © 1974 by Marchette Chute. Reprinted by permission of the publisher, E.P. Dutton, a division of New American Library and the author.

Page 235: From "Little Otter's Coasting Party" in *Little Otter Remembers and Other Stories* by Ann Tompert. Text copyright © 1977 by Ann Tompert. Used by permission of Crown Publishers, Inc.

Artists

Reading Warm-up: Frank Asch

Section 1: Andrea Eberbach, 18–19; Karen Hahn, 16–17; Janet LaSalle, 41; David Povilaitis, 20; Larry Mikec, 35–39

Section 2: Andrea Eberbach, 52–56; John Faulkner, 83; Robert Masheris, 81; Phil Renaud, 57, 58, 59, 61–66, 68; George Suyeoka, 89

Section 3: Andrea Eberbach, 96–98; Marlene Ekman, 124, 126–133; Luke More, 135; David Povilaitis, 123; Phil Renaud, 99–108; George Suyeoka, 135; Robert Wahlgren, (border art), 125–133

Section 4: Franz Altschuler, 176; Ralph Creasman, 163; Pat Dypold, 165–174; Andrea Eberbach, 164; John Faulkner, 136, 137; George Suyeoka, 139–140; Ed Tabor, 156–161; Robert Wahlgren, 141–145, 146–149

Section 5: Andrea Eberbach, 180–182; Judith Friedman, 187–191; Kees de Kiefte, 183–186; Janet LaSalle, 216; Helen Nelson Reed, 193–201, 203, 204; Robert Wahlgren, 209, 211, 217

Section 6: John Michael Downs, 240–244; Andrea Eberbach, 220; James Higa, 234; Laurie Jordan, 246–256; Robert Masheris, 218; Steve Schindler, 235–239; George Suyeoka, 259; Robert Wahlgren, 221, 222, 228, 231, 232

Glossary: George Suyeoka

Photographs

Page 29: Courtesy Harper & Row, Publishers, Inc.; Page 31: Hans Reinhard/BRUCE COLEMAN INC., New York; Page 32: (top) © New York Zoological Society; Pages 32–33: (bottom) Alexander Lowry/National Audubon Society Collection/Photo Researchers; Page 33: (top left) Neg. no. 123576 (Photo: Rota) Courtesy Dept. Library Services, American Museum of Natural History; Page 33: (top right) Neg. no. 124861 (Photo: Rota) Courtesy Dept. Library Services, American Museum of Natural History; Page 34: H. Charles Laun/National Audubon Society Collection/Photo Researchers; Page 85: Joseph A. Di Chello Jr.; Page 86: (left) Dean Abramson; Page 87: (left) Marbeth © 1985; Page 87: (right) © Rhoda Baer; Page 88, 90 (right), 91 (bottom): Photos by Art Pahlke. Courtesy ANIMART, INC., Chicago, IL; Page 90: (left) Franz Altschuler; Page 91: (top) M. Timothy O'Keefe/BRUCE COLEMAN INC., New York; Page 91: (center) Sandy Macys/TAURUS PHOTOS, INC.; Pages 94–95: Owen Franken/Stock, Boston; Page 121: Courtesy Albert Whitman & Company; Page 135: Franz Altschuler; Page 138: Walter Chandoha; Page 141: (right) Courtesy Macmillan Publishing Company; Pages 141–145: © 1982 by Carol Lea Benjamin, reprinted by permission of Harper & Row, Publishers, Inc.; Pages 178–179: Franz Altschuler; Pages 206–207: ANIMALS ANIMALS/Richard Kolar; Page 208: Mark Newman/TOM STACK & ASSOCIATES; Pages 209: Wilbur S. Tripp/Photo Researchers; Page 210: Wayne Lankinen/BRUCE COLEMAN INC., New York; Page 211: Leonard Lee Rue III/National Audubon Society/Photo Researchers; Page 212: Dr. Fred J. Alsop/BRUCE COLEMAN INC., New York; Page 213: (left) ANIMALS ANIMALS/Perry Slocum; Page 213: (right) ANIMALS ANIMALS/John Trott; Page 214: Steve Maslowski/Photo Researchers; Page 217: James P. Rowan; Pages 229–231: Art Pahlke for Scott, Foresman; Page 234: Photo by Congrat-Butlar. Courtesy E.P. Dutton & Co.; Page 257: Historical Pictures Service, Chicago.

Cover Artist
Karen Hahn